WELCOME TO A FARE CHANCE

"**A FARE CHANCE** is for He and She who either don't know how to cook, have limited time, want to be more organized in their kitchen or crave a new stance on cooking. Whether you are a motivated novice ready to begin a culinary journey or a connoisseur seeking a culinary avant-garde you will have fun and be entertained.

A FARE CHANCE is full of vintage to modern day simple recipes and effortless tips created through love, fun, and thankful festivities. My adorable man and I are posed throughout the book to create amusing moments partner with a play on words type writing.

A FARE CHANCE is unpretentious and exciting; as a matter of fact, the recipes are written like most family recipes. Take a cooking moment to relish in the fare!"

Colleen C. Carson

CARSON POWER PRODUCTIONS
Vancouver, B. C.

Cover Design by Graphic Designer | Frina Art

Book Design by Author | Colleen C. Carson
(www.theguyedbook.com)

Editor | Catherine Carrington

Author's Back Cover Photo | Photographer | Charles Zuckermann Photography
(www.charleszuckermann.com)

A Fare Chance Copyright ©2007 Colleen C. Carson

A Fare Chance Revised Copyright ©2019 Colleen C. Carson

ALL RIGHTS RESERVED.
This book contains material protected under International
and Federal Copyright Laws and Treaties.

Any unauthorized reprint or use of this material is prohibited. No part of this Book may be reproduced or transmitted in any form or by any means, electronic or mechanical, including photocopying, recording, or by any information storage and retrieval system without express wrote/written permission from the author/publisher.

Colleen C. Carson

My Dearest Fare,

Our relationship goes back decades, but it seems like yesterday. You presented yourself in such a teasing manner when observed along with an enticing show of desirables. I knew on meeting we would be together forever it was love at first nibble and it's been a love of fare since and forever.

Together we have planned such celebrations as births, weddings, anniversaries, even remembrances with tender morsels to share. You have presented stirring savvies and bathed moments of essences which we both relished.

My fare, over the years you have been obliging in wanting to please my kneads! Your saucy appeal, catered rubs, and delicate bites of pleasure have without question spiced up my life while measuring up to all my expectations. Of course, in all relationships, there have been times where you were quite braising, leaving me stewing for hours! On occasion, your indulgence has stirred up several to sear or reach their boiling point yet, in the end, you were always about being fare.

Remember, when we started our business together, it was somewhat intimidating, but due to teamwork, careful attention, and of course our creations; we achieved success. Even when others differed in mindset or took you for granted, you were able to just toss their thoughts aside. Sometimes it grates on me how others have no time or don't even want to try to see how you could blend in their lives. It doesn't seem to batter you; I know I must stop simmering over grating situations.

We have had very steamy moments of unforgettable along with simmering instances of inviting display while blending well in creativity, which I'm genuinely thankful. I believe our journey has many more creations to share and my interest awe-inspiring. Enclosing I want to say, to you, my dearest fare...

"Romance is like vegetables better when fresh."

"DEDICATION TO MY MOM,
DAUGHTER CRYSTAL, SON CHANCE,
MY DONALD, CHOSEN FAMILY, AND FRIENDS;
FOREVER ALWAYS CHERISHED MEMORIES."

"Men like the smell of yeast because it reminds them of Beer."

MEET THE CHEF

Colleen has been preparing food, creating recipes, and entertaining for over fifty years in her passion for culinary pleasure shared with loved ones and others. She had her catering and event business for more than 18 years in Vancouver; where she served the rich and famous, national leaders, and representatives, on and off movie sets, families celebrating a birth, marriage, and intimate dinners of romantic bliss.

Her earliest memories of cooking began watching her Mom in the kitchen, preparing meals, canning fruits, pickles, jellies, and baking loaves of bread. Colleen would ask her Mom questions about the why and what about cooking and her Mom would patiently reply to her attentive daughter.

One day Colleen came home from school, and as always snacks were waiting for Colleen and her sisters to consume as if they hadn't eaten all day. Colleen's Mom asked her if she would like to help prepare dinner, and with an enthusiastic reply, Colleen said, "Yes!" As her sisters played in the backyard, she assisted her Mom in cooking her favourite meal, a tomato and cheese pasta dish.

Colleen's assistance in the preparation of meals continued, which was pleasing because she was learning the enjoyment of cooking and creating meals. Then, her Mom told her that she could prepare a Sunday dinner on her own, which brought an array of emotions from the excitement of anticipation. If you can remember back in the sixties Sunday was always about the succulent roast with roasted to perfection vegetables and potatoes accompanied by either Yorkshire pudding or freshly baked bread, along with the finger dipping gravy, and of course the pretentious Sunday dessert.

Colleen remembers she felt incredibly obliging yet anxious at that moment of her Mom's invite. But then she thought, "I have been waiting for this time to prove I can cook a family meal on my own, and I know I can do it!" She remembers anxiously awaiting dinner to be served to receive the accolades from her Mom, Dad, and sisters. They started coming immediately on consumption, allowing her to feel very accomplished in the art of cooking. As years past Colleen was creating recipes, whether it be a culinary dish or a marinade concoction; she would always await a response from her sampler's. Realizing cooking was her haven of creativity accompanied by the solace of thoughts, anticipation, and accomplishment, she was living her passion.

Colleen expressed, "My Mom ignited my passion for cooking!" She continued, "Cooking is about taking chances in expressing yourself through food, some of the best recipes in the world started as an idea with an intuitive apprehension thus 'A Fare Chance.' The enjoyment and indulgence from family and friends are pleasing, and their expression of thank you is also rewarding. Food is a living influence that brings us together in the way of sharing laughter, spoken thoughts, and best of all; love!"

"Bananas make other fruits ripen because of releasing a gas called ethene. Placing the unripe with a banana in a brown bag speeds up the ripening process."

INTRODUCTION

'A Fare Chance' cookbook is about giving you a fair chance at learning how to cook or enhancing your culinary skill! My collection of vintage family recipes created over these last fifty years for family, friends, and my catering company are easy and rewarding.

I have created these recipes with a dash of easy, a tablespoon of simple, a squeeze of gourmet, a drizzle of humour, a sprinkle of romance, and several cups of love. I have created menus for each night of the week that will wow you in the simplicity and easy preparation along with an unforgettable culinary experience for loved ones! One of my pet peeve's with cookbooks is when I want to increase the volume of ingredients or add a new element; there's no space to do so. 'A Fare Chance' has left an area for you to write information on whether increasing the volume, improvising or adding a new ingredient.

I love gazing at the food images in a cookbook on a rainy afternoon with a cup of coffee, don't you? Once finished, I put the cookbook back on the shelf rarely ever preparing a recipe within it because I've never been of the mindset to set one's self up for failure. 'A Fare Chance' has no food images because it's about you having fun cooking not wondering if it's going to have the same appearance as a photo that was styled by a professional food stylist. Look, cooking is supposed to be about your creativity and having the mindset of fun and adventure. I have images in this book but their fun and far from intimidating.

Why was 'A Fare Chance' written? When my children moved out and settled, they realized I was the matriarch of the family recipes. Constant phone calls for recipes became the norm until one day my son, Chance, asked if I would write my recipes into a cookbook format so they would have a copy of them.

Of course, I agreed and began organizing my recipes into a cookbook and on Mother's Day of 2007 gave a copy each to Crystal and Chance as a gift of thank you for allowing me the privilege of being called their Mom. I can't begin to tell you how happy I was to have achieved my son's request because, on July 28, 2007, my son, Chance passed away suddenly. If you've been looking for a cookbook that will bring laughter, fun, and luscious moments of culinary delight; "A FARE CHANCE" is the cookbook for YOU!

"The single most powerful weapon against food borne illness: hand washing."

"As a child, the kitchen was the heart of our home; it always had a comforting mood on a winter dusk or a fresh feel on a summer morn. A room full of tempting aromas, collective tasting, fun conversation, and various songs, but the best of the kitchen had been always Mom. Now, as a Mom, much has not changed, but now the best in my kitchen are my family and friends!"

20 TOP LURING APHRODISIAC'S

Champagne
Red Wine
Oysters
Garlic
Salmon
Coffee
Chocolate
Bananas
Avocadoes
Hot Chilies
Cherries
Strawberries
Honey
Whipping Cream
Pumpkin
Vanilla
Figs
Almonds/Walnuts
Ginseng
Saffron

TABLE OF CONTENTS

FARE ADVICE 1
Forms of Cooking 3
Food & Freezing Tips 4
Food safety suggestions 5
When in Season 6
Let's Talk Oil 7
Let's Talk Servings 8
Food Pantry Essentials 9
Must Have Herbs & Spices 9
Fridge Staples 10
Must-Have Kitchenware 11
Imperial & Metric Conversion 12

SAVOIR FARE 17
Social Styling 19
Wine Pairing 21
Fare Issensual 28
Table Setting for Home Dining 30
Table Centerpiece 31
Dining Ambiance 32

VANITY FARE 35
Awe Shucks I Love You 37
Let's Do Picnic in the Pork 38
Steak With Me Sweet Mirin 39
Crudo's to Us 40
Don't Be Bleu We Can Still Brie Friends 41

You Mushroom My Inspiration 42
Wasa And Sashi are Soya Happy 43
Let's Scallop into the Sunset 44
Salmon Else Loves Her Loxs 45
Don't Be Crabby Spread the Love 46
You Spice Up My Life 47
Put a Wing on it 48
You are Crabulous 49
Keep it Shrimple Sweetheart 50
Things Could Get Steamy 51
You are my Tunacorn 52
Your Love is Unshellfish 53
Olive of Me Loves Olive of You 54

FARE SHARE **57**
I'm Tongue Thai Over You 59
I'm Appley to Know You Sugar 60
I Knew You Would be Truffle 61
I Appeachiate You Baby 62
To My Dearest Clove 63
You're a Fine Cookie 64
Leeks Reveal You're a Spud..65
I'm Sweet Over You Puddin 66
I Yam Wanting You 67
Thanks for Pudding Me First 68
Peas Be My Chicky-Boo.. 69
You Make My Life Pearfect 70
You're Souper Hot 71
I'm Berry Much in Love With You 72

FARE HAND **75**

    You Shrimply Guac My World 77
    The Flower Of My Life 78
    Mr. Cuke Rode Off on His Scallion 79
    You are My Slham Dunk 80
    He Spudder Her Name Baconing My Heart 81
    My Ramentic Ways are So Hot 82
    My Tunaverse has Always Been You 83
    Our Hearts Romaine in Love 84
    You are the Star in My Life 85
    We Have the Slaw of Attraction 86
    Celerybrating the Pastability of Forever Love 87

FARE PLAY **89**

    Ms. Rice rumored in a spanish a fare 91
    Would be Grate If We Do Dinner Tomato 92
    If You're Chili I Know How to Heat You Up 93
    Mr. Shep Herd I Only Have Pies for You 94
    My Chick Was Stewing for Hours 95
    My Misteak was not Loving Vegie More 96
    Pastably a Weekend at My Cottage 97
    Rooting for Me is Better than Wineing 98
    Bella Want to Meat Mr. Rice Guy 99
    Prawnise I Won't Bacon Your Heart 100
    You Rib Me About Your Saucy Way 101
    It's Offishial I Want To Mayo You 102
    Our Love Has Mushroom Over the Years 103
    I'm Soya Nuts Over You 104
    You're Salmon to Adough 105
    Pastabiliy You'll Bake My Heart 106
    You're Salmon Whose Butter than Me........................... 107

Your Spicy Scent is Seducing 108
Taco 'Bout Loving You 109
I Steak My Heart on Your Love 110
You Leave Me Speachless 111

FAMILY AFFARE 113

Canadiana Dinner 117
Parisian Dinner 119
Italian Dinner 121
Grecian Dinner 123
Americana Dinner 126
Asian Dinner 128
Sunday Brunch 130
Family Fare Dinner 134
Infamous Roast Beef Dinner 136

FOOD FOR THOUGHT 139

Appetizers 139
Soups 140
Desserts 140
Salads 141

"IT'S EASY AND FUN!"

It began with two empty wine glasses
A park in the early evening
A blanket sprawled with my favourite tastes
He childlike in the feat of my amaze

This is only the beginning he recited
While feeding me in delightful bites
Sipping on our wine of choice
And my thoughts of his perfection

FARE ADVICE

A FARE CHANCE

FARE ADVICE

FORMS OF COOKING

Blanching: You put vegetables or fruit into boiling water for 2 to 3 minutes, then remove and immediately put into ice-filled water.

Braising: Put the meat in hot oil or fat; brown the meat on all sides before pouring any liquid in for stewing or roasting.

Simmering: You cook the food in hot liquids. The temperature is just below the boiling point (100°C) or set at low. It's a slower method of cooking.

Steaming: When steaming, you don't use liquid, just steam; boil water in a pot or a double boiler. Place the food in a colander type container which will let through the steam, and place on the boiling water pot and cover.

Stewing: The meat must be braised, first, then add your diced vegetables. Add you're liquid whether a broth, wine or beer, bring to a boil, then lower temperature to a low to medium and cover for about one hour, this allows the meat to become tender and juicy.

Deep Frying: Submerge the food into the hot oil. It's very fast. It's vital the oil is very hot. Put three popcorn kernels in the oil as it heats. The popcorn will pop when the oil is between 350°F and 365°F, the perfect temperature for deep frying.

Pan Frying: A little cooking oil or fat is used to cover the base of the frying pan. Both sides of the food must be fried.

Sauté: Use just a little oil or fat in a shallow pan on high heat. The food must be kept moving. Toss the food on all sides. It's a fast method of cooking. Brown the food, but remember to keep the colour, moisture, and flavour intact.

Grilling: This means cooking food under direct heat like barbequing. It is the same form of cooking as pan frying only you are cooking on a grill.

Baking: The food is put into an oven where heat and time are regulated to cook the food to perfection.

Stewing: Food is cooked using a lot of liquid. There's usually a combination of vegetables and meat put into a liquid base that cooks slowly over a couple of hours. Fruits are stewed for some desserts.

Boiling: This is a method of cooking that is quite simple. The water is heated while the food in the water cooks. The excess water can either be thrown away or added to the meat drippings to make gravy. With rice, the liquid is usually absorbed.

Roasting: When heat is applied to the outer part of the food, it seals it up, thereby trapping all the juices inside the food and causing a crispy crust on the outer part of the food and allows the food to cook evenly.

Basting: The juice of the meat is ladled over the meat frequently while it is roasting.

FOOD & FREEZING TIPS

Ripening Tomatoes: Seal in a brown paper bag with an apple or pear, which produces a natural gas that speeds up ripening

How to cook hard boiled eggs: Arrange eggs in a single layer. Pour cold water an inch above eggs. Cover & Bring to a boil over high heat, remove immediately and let stand for 20 minutes.

Peeling eggs: Hold under cold running water while peeling

Bean Sprouts make much better eating if the root ends are pinched off soaking the sprouts in cold water, crisps them and removes any stale taste left over from the sprouting water.

Gravy Tip: To darken light gravy, add 1 Tsp. to 1 Tbsp. of instant coffee

Avocado Tip: When making guacamole to keep it from going brown put the seed in the center of the mix.

Removing skin from roasted peppers: Place in a paper bag for 5 to 7 minutes, then rub the bag against the pepper.

Quick Tenderizer: Add a tablespoon of vinegar to the water when boiling meat or ribs; it will help tenderize even the toughest meat

Wilted Vegetables: Soak wilted veggies in two cups water, one tablespoon vinegar to help bring them back to life.

Refreezing Fruits: Only if they taste and smell good.

Frozen Dinners: Do not refreeze frozen dinners. Thawed frozen foods and frozen meals should be cooked immediately.

Vegetables: Do not refreeze thawed vegetables, as the bacteria in these foods multiply rapidly. Spoilage may begin before bad odours develop and may be very toxic. Refreeze vegetables only if ice crystals remain throughout the package. If you question the condition, **THROW THEM OUT.**

Meat and Poultry: Becomes unsafe to eat when they start to spoil. Check each package of thawed meat or poultry for any offensive odour then discard the meat. Immediately cook when thawed.

Fish and Shellfish: Do not re-freeze unless ice crystals remain throughout the package. Seafood may be spoiled even if it has no offensive odour.

Ice Cream: Do not refreeze melted ice cream.

FOOD SAFETY SUGGESTIONS

It is vitally important to keep foods safe to eat. Here are some helpful tips:

A. Invest in a freezer and refrigerator thermometer to store food safely:
- Your refrigerator temperature should be at 40°F (4.44°C) or below.
- Keep your freezer temperature below 0°F (17.8°C).
- Keep your refrigerator and freezer no more than 75% full to work efficiently; this leaves room for air to circulate.

B. Cook foods to their proper internal temperature:
- 145°F (62.8°C) Beef, lamb & veal steaks & roasts, medium rare
- 160°F (71.1°C) Beef, lamb & veal steaks & roasts, medium
- 145°F (62.8°C) Fish
- 160°F (71.1°C) Ground beef, pork, veal & lamb; chops, ribs & roasts
- 165°F (73.9°C) Ground turkey & chicken. Stuffing & casseroles
- 170°F (76.7°C) Chicken & turkey breasts
- 180°F (82.2°C) Chicken & turkey, whole bird, legs, thighs & wings

C. Keep cold foods COLD and hot foods HOT:
- The food temperature danger zone is between 41°F and 141°F (5°C and 51°C) Bacteria grows rapidly between these temperatures
- Discard any food left out at room temperature for more than two hours. Discard after one hour if the temperature was above 90°F (32.2°C).
- Place leftovers into shallow containers and immediately put them in the refrigerator or freezer for rapid cooling. (It's a common fallacy that food should be cooled at room temperature before refrigerating!)
- Reheat any leftovers to an internal temperature of 165°F (73.9°C).

WHEN IN SEASON

Apples	July to October
Asparagus	March to May
Apricots	July to August
Beets	June to August
Blueberries	July to September
Broccoli	September to November
Brussels Sprout	September to February
Carrots (baby)	July to September
Cabbage	August to November
Cauliflower	August to October
Celery	July to October
Cherries	June to August
Corn on the Cob	August to September
Cucumbers	July to September
Garlic	September to November
Ginger	September to November
Green/Yellow Beans	July to September
Kale	September to April
Leeks	September to March
Lettuce	June to September
Mushrooms	Year-round
Nugget Potatoes	June to August
Potatoes	September to December
Onions (Green)	June to September
Onions	Year-round
Peaches	Aug to September
Pears	Aug to September
Peas	June to September
Peppers	June to August
Plums	August to September
Radishes	June to August
Raspberries	June to August
Spinach	June to August
Squash	September to October
Strawberries	June to August
Tomatoes	June to August
Turnip	December to February
Zucchini	June to August

LET'S TALK OIL

First, what does 'Oil Smoke Point' mean?

The smoke point generally refers to the temperature at which a cooking fat or oil begins to break down to glycerol and free fatty acids (FFA) and produce bluish smoke. The smoke point also marks the beginning of both flavour and nutritional degradation. Therefore, it is a key consideration when selecting a fat for frying, with the smoke point of the specific oil dictating its maximum usable temperature and thus its possible applications. For instance, since deep frying is a very high-temperature process, it requires fat with a high smoke point (Wikipedia 2011).

Here is a list of Oils and their smoke point:

OILS	F	C
Almond Oil	420	216
Avocado Oil	520	271
Butter	350	177
Butter (Ghee)	485	252
Canola Oil	400	204
Coconut Oil	350	177
Corn Oil	320	160
Flaxseed Oil	225	107
Grapeseed Oil	435	223
Hazelnut Oil	430	223
Hemp Seed Oil	330	165
Olive Oil (Virgin)	400	204
Palm Oil	450	232
Peanut Oil	450	232
Rice Brand Oil	495	257
Safflower Oil	450	232
Sesame Oil	400	204
Sunflower Oil	390	199
Vegetable Oil	450	232
Walnut Oil	320	160

Refined and filtered oils are the best for frying because they withstand heat for prolonged periods. Olive and Sesame Oils are two of the most ancient oils, dating back more than 4000 years. Most above are cold-pressed oils which are mostly used for cooking.

LET'S TALK SERVINGS

APPETIZERS
- 4-6 servings per person preceding a meal @ three-hour duration
- 10-12 servings per person as a meal @ three-hour duration
- Dips & Spreads – 1 ounce per serving
- Fillers-always have these choices as well; peanuts, chips, pretzels, etc.
- An option is to serve bread and two salads along with appetizers as a meal

RULE OF THUMB
- Up to 50 people: 5 to 6 varieties
- 50 to 100 people: 7 to 8 varieties
- More than 100: 8 to 10 varieties

BEVERAGES
- Soft Drinks — 2-8 ounce serving per hour
- Punch — 2-4 ounce serving per hour
- Tea — 2-8 ounce serving per hour
- Coffee — 2-4 ounce serving per hour
- Alcohol — 1-1½ drinks per hour
- Water — Always 2 Pitchers

ENTRÉE
- Poultry & Fish — 6-8 ounces
- Red Meat — 14-16 ounces
- Roast — 8-10 ounces
- Ribs — 1 pound
- Soup/Stew — 1 cup @ the first course and 2 cups @ the main course
- Rice, Grains — 2-3 ounces
- Potatoes — Medium to Large
- Vegetables — 4 ounces
- Beans — 2 ounces
- Pasta — 2-3 ounces for a first course
- Pasta — 4-5 ounces for a main dish
- Pasta — 1 pound serves 3-4 people
- Green Salad — 1.5 cups
- Head of Lettuce — 4-5 people
- Bread — 1 slice per person

DESSERTS
- 1 Slice — pastry
- 1 Cup — creamy dessert (example: ice cream)

FARE ADVICE

FOOD PANTRY ESSENTIALS

Canola Oil	Olive Oil
Vinegar	Worcestershire Sauce
Mustard	Dijon Mustard
Barbeque Sauce	Soya Sauce
Chicken Broth	Beef Broth
Cream Soups	Can Mushrooms
Hot Sauce	Ketchup
Lime Juice	Lemon Juice
Coffee	Tea
Syrup	Cocoa
White Sugar	Brown Sugar
Salt	Pepper
Flour	Pasta
Can Tomatoes	Salsa
Peanut Butter	Jam
Crackers	Breadcrumbs
Rice	Potatoes
Onions	Garlic

MUST HAVE HERBS & SPICES

Allspice – Sweet & Strong. Relish, pickle, fruit preserve, desserts.

Anise – Licorice-like. Meats, veggies, candy, dessert.

Basil – Pungent, Sweet. Stuffing, pasta, dressing, fish, meats, sauces.

Bay Leaf – Strong & Pungent. Stew, soup, pickles, sauces, marinades.

Caraway – Sweet & Sharp. Meat loaves, stew, pot roast, bread, sauces, veggies.

Cardamom – Pungent & Aromatic. Bread, desserts, meats, & fish.

Cayenne – Hot & Spicy. Meats, seafood, soup, dips, spreads, and cheese dishes.

Celery Salt – Tangy & Savoury. Caesar Drink, stew, fish, stuffing, and meats.

Chili Powder – Hot & Peppery. Latin food, beans, rice, sauces, and egg dishes.

Cinnamon – Sweet & Spicy. Best in desserts, veggies, beverages, sauces.

Cloves – Strong & Sweet. Pork, lamb, relish, pickle, fruits, and desserts.

Coriander – Sage & Lemon. Curry, stew, pickles, rice, desserts, gingerbread.

Cumin – Strong & Bitter. Eastern, Spanish, Mexican dishes, tomato dishes.

Curry Powder – Warm & Sharp. Meats, seafood, rice, sauces, soups.

Dill Weed – Mild, Versatile. Soup, dressing, fish, meats, pickles.
Ginger – Pungent & Spicy. Asian dishes, meats, fruits, veggies, desserts, jam.
Mace – Like Nutmeg. Veal, fish, stew, egg, cheese, soups, desserts, veggies.
Marjoram – Spicy & Sweet. Meats, fish, stew, casseroles, gravy, salad, egg.
Mint – Spicy & Cool. Lamb, beef, relishes, jelly, fruit, sauces, veggies, salad.
Mustard – Pungent & Sour. Pickle, relish, dressing, marinade, ham, corn-beef.
Nutmeg – Sweet & Spicy. Veggies, egg dishes, beverage, desserts, sauces, breads.
Oregano – Strong, Aromatic. Pasta, pizza, dressings, soups, meats, seafood.
Paprika – Mild & Sweet. Meats, dressing, dips, salads, veggies, soup.
Parsley – Mild, Versatile. Garnish, non-sweet foods.
Poultry Seasoning – Mild & Sage-like. Poultry, stuffing, biscuits.
Rosemary – Sweet, Spicy. Stews, casseroles, stuffing, breads, meats, fish.
Saffron – Strong & Bitter. Poultry, fish, seafood, rice, bread, cakes.
Sage – Strong & Bitter. Meats, fish, stuffing, veggies, gravy, sauces.
Savoury – Mild & Peppery. Meats, fish, coup, stuffing, sauces, egg dishes.
Seasoning Salt – Savoury & Versatile. Everything other than sweets.
Sesame Seeds – Nutlike & Mild. Garnish, breads, rolls, cookies, salad.
Tarragon – Mild & Licorice-like. Meats, fish, stew, veggies, salad, sauces.
Thyme – Strong, Pungent. Meats, stews, sauces, fish, veggies, dressings.
Turmeric – Pepperlike & Bitter. Curry, pickle, relish, dressings, dips.

FRIDGE STAPLES

Milk	Butter
Mayonnaise	Sour Cream
Dijon Mustard	Yogurt
Eggs	Orange Juice
Ginger	Feta Cheese
Cheddar Cheese	Parmesan Cheese
Vegetables	Fruit

These selections are based on most people's cooking uses, but again you can personalize to your taste preferences.

MUST-HAVE KITCHENWARE

Dishes & Cutlery
- Coffee Mugs or Cups & Saucers (or both)
- 12-16 Drinking Glasses
- 10-12 Wine Glasses
- 8-10 Dinner Plates
- 8-10 Side Plates
- 8-10 Soup Bowls
- 12-16 Knives, Forks, Salad Forks, Soup Spoons & Dessert Spoons
- Serving Trays---six varying sizes
- Serving or Mixing Bowls---six different sizes
- Salt & Pepper Shakers
- Set of Steak Knives
- Set of Carving Knives

Cookware & Appliances
- Frying Pans Large, Medium & Small
- 2 Dutch Oven
- 5 Saucepans 2 Large, 2 Medium & Small
- Toaster
- Microwave
- Coffee Brewer
- Electric Beaters
- Blender

Utensils
- Can Opener
- Corkscrew
- Measuring Cups & Spoons
- 2 Strainers---1 large for salads & 1 small for straining
- Spatula
- Potato Peeler
- Grater
- Pizza Wheel
- Potato Masher
- Garlic Press
- 2 Large Serving Forks & Spoons---1 slotted
- Flipper or Turner
- Wire Whisk
- Large Scissors
- 2-4 Candle Holders
- Tongs

IMPERIAL & METRIC CONVERSION

VOLUME CONVERSION	
Imperial	**Metric**
1/4 tsp. (teaspoon)	1.25 ml (milliliter)
1/2 tsp.	2.5 ml
1 tsp.	5.0 ml
1 tbsp. (tablespoon)	15 ml
1/4 cup	60 ml
1/3 cup	75 ml
1/2 cup	125 ml
2/3 cup	150 ml
3/4 cup	175 ml
1 cup	250 ml
1 1/8 cups	275 ml
1 1/4 cups	300 ml
1 1/2 cups	350 ml
1 2/3 cups	400 ml
1 3/4 cups	450 ml
2 cups	500 ml
2 1/2 cups	600 ml
3 cups	750 ml
3 2/3 cups	900 ml
4 cups	1000 ml or 1 liter

OVEN CONVERSION		
Fahrenheit	**Celsius**	**Oven Heat**
225°	110°	very cool
250°	120°	very cool
275°	140°	cool
300°	150°	cool
325°	160°	moderate
350°	180°	moderate
375°	190°	moderately hot
400°	200°	moderately hot
425°	220°	hot
450°	230°	very hot

FARE ADVICE

LENGTH CONVERSION	
Imperial	**Metric**
1/4 in (inch)	5 mm (millimeter)
1/2 in	1 cm (centimeter)
1 in	2.5 cm
2 in	5 cm
3 in	7 cm
4 in	10 cm
5 in	12 cm
6 in	15 cm
7 in	18 cm
8 in	20 cm
9 in	23 cm
10 in	25 cm
11 in	28 cm
12 in (1 foot)	30 cm

WEIGHT CONVERSION	
Imperial	**Metric**
1/2 oz. (ounce)	15 g (grams)
1 oz.	25 g
2 oz.	50 g
3 oz.	75 g
4 oz.	100 g
6 oz.	175 g
7 oz.	200 g
8 oz.	250 g
9 oz.	275 g
10 oz.	300 g
12 oz.	350 g
1 lb. (pound)	500 g
1 1/2	750 g
2 lb.	1 kg (kilogram)

FARE   **RULE**

Flavorful cuisine and cocktails
Astonishing hostess and/or host to orchestrate
Reminiscing on times now and then
Entertaining adorable family and friends

FARE ADVICE

A FARE CHANCE

SAVOIR FARE

A FARE CHANCE

SAVOIR FARE

SOCIAL STYLING

Social styling is not your guest's fashion statement; it's the mode of culinary fashion you create with such features as lighting, sound, seating, and fare. A dinner or cocktail party designed to enhance your style of entertaining personality; it allows your guests to feel comfortable even if this is the first time, they have had the opportunity to meet you. I would say there are social styles that are used most often when entertaining; Cocktail Party, Bohemian Sharing, and Romantic Dining.

MÉLANGE is a party at which cocktails & bite-size food is served. Midday to early evening is the usual time.

BOHEMIAN is a meal where you share food. Sometimes this type of meal is last minute or planned with a theme. Brunch to Dinner is likely time slots.

ROMANTIC is a dinner which is lit by candles to create a romantic mood. Styling a table with an elegant motif rather than classic can also be thought of as romantic. Romance is welcome any time of the day.

Let's begin with lighting. Fashion your home with lamp lighting and accessorize with an array of candles creating a warm and welcoming ambiance for your guests. No overhead lighting it tends to distract and unease your guests.

Music styles the mood of your guest's background is where it stays for conversations to flow. I got a bit of an education on this point when a dinner guest asked if I could change the jazz music I had on. She said that she found the unresolved tension of the jazz chords distracting. When I listened for a few minutes, I realized she had a point. I may have loved the music, but it was drawing attention to itself. I was wrong to assume that it worked well for a dinner party.

Classical music is always a good choice. If you choose music with vocal, be careful to keep it unobtrusive, a conversation should still be the priority. If styling a theme for your social than the choice of music would outfit the idea.

Seating your guests for a dinner party should be planned, announcing to your guests to sit wherever it usually makes them feel awkward. It is customary to separate couples, along with male than female around the table. Don't place things on the table like purses or cell phones, and cell phones should be on silent during the dinner.

A cocktail party is the opposite in seating. The less seating, the more movement you will have among your guest's which creates a flare of excitement.

A Styled Cocktail Social

A Prepared Cocktail to open the evening: Address your guests about the evening's Fare while serving a tantalizing cocktail. The cocktail is usually 30 minutes before serving the appetizers, whether a dinner or cocktail party.

A Runway of Culinary Collections: Hot & Cold Appetizers equally, an array of delectable appetizers designed to enlighten the palate. During the dinner hours, you would allow for 12 to 14 appetizers per guest if afternoon or late evening then 6 to 8 appetizers per guest. Dessert would be served later the dessert table, 2 to 3 pieces per guest.

A Styled Dinner Social

A Prepared Cocktail to open the evening: address your guests about the evening's Fare while serving a tantalizing cocktail. A vodka base is a trend and fashionable. The cocktail is usually 30 minutes before serving the appetizers. The appetizers are 45 to 60 minutes before the first course. When coming to the end of the 60 minutes, your guests would move to the styled seating to be served.

The First Course the Soup: whether a creamy chilled bisque or warm medley chowder, a serving should only be a cup in volume. From May until early September a cold soup is recommended. Consuming will take about 25 to 30 minutes.

The Second Course the Salad: A cup of fresh, crisp greens accessorized with roasted nuts, berries and accents of cheese dressed in vintage marinate.

After the Salad allows for a 20 minutes break in preparation of the Entrée.

The Entrée: A delicious red or white meat of choice or enticing morsels of Seafood/Fish partnered with an array of trendy in-vogue vegetables.

The Finale: A dessert connoisseur's palate, finishing with a rich and pleasing coffee.

"Social styling should create the essence of memorable, a model of lasting ambiance, and a culinary runway of vintage or contemporary Fare for you and your guests to reminisce."

WINE PAIRING

There are two items as guidelines for matching your food and wine: the weight and flavour of your culinary choice.

Weight for wines just refers to alcohol content:
- Light means about 8% to 10%
- Medium-bodied means about 10.5% to 12%
- Full-bodied means about 12.5% to 16%

The next consideration is the essence of your dish:
- The sweet fare should be matched with sweet wine, an ice or sparkling wine.
- The lighter, delicate fare should be matched with an acidic wine, a white or rosé.
- The savoury or robust fare should be matched with an intense wine, like red wine.

How much should I spend?

Some of the best wines I have tasted have been in the $25 to $40 range.

What kind of wine glasses should I use?

- Red wines are full-bodied in character; a large bowl-shaped glass will allow it to breathe.
- White wine is cold and refreshing; a medium bowl-shaped glass keeps it cool longer.
- Champagne is bubbly; champagne flutes are tall and thin, allowing the inspection of colour, and movement of the bubbles. All wines should be served in a delicate type of stemware.

What temperature should the wine be at?

- Aged red wines: 16-17 °C
- Young reds: 14-16 °C
- Rosés: 10-12 °C
- Whites: 8-10 °C
- Aged whites: 10-12 °C
- Sparkling wines: 7-10 °C
- Dessert wines: 7-8 °C
- Dry generous wines: 7 °C
- Ice wine is best served at 12°C

If you chill a wine much below these temperatures' guidelines, you risk compromising both flavour and balance. Should I let the wine breathe?

There is no need to let chilled white wines breathe you should open red wine about half an hour before serving or use a decanter or an aerator. This allows the air to get in and bring out the bouquet and flavour. Should I serve the wine my guest brought? The wine your guest brings is a gift; it is up to you whether to serve it or not. If you have carefully paired your fare and wine, then put it aside for another time. If your guest is offended, you can always serve it before or after dinner.

Selecting a wine that is a compliment to your fare can be accomplished easily if you know. I am giving you a primer for this knowledge in a natural learnable form; when entertaining, share this knowledge with your guest/guests for their amusement and appreciation.

WHITE WINES

Chardonnay
- a green-skinned grape variety used to make white wine
- originated in the Burgundy wine region of eastern France
- is now grown from England to New Zealand
- tends to be medium to light body
- is an important component of many sparkling wines including Champagne
- pairs with fish/seafood, salads, soups, chicken, veal

Chablis wine
- richness that is widely planted and tends to reveal a California quality
- thrives in a variety of climates
- fruity and rich
- most popular
- in-demand grape varieties
- reliably pleasing flavours
- pairs with a wide range of foods especially oysters, fish/seafood, sauces, dairy

Chenin Blanc
- has been blended with honey and flowers
- high levels of acidity
- is grown in France, California, Australia, New Zealand, and South Africa
- absolutely delicious
- pairs with salads, soups, fish/seafood, chicken

Gewürztraminer:
- deeply colored, full-flavored, highest alcohol-content white wine in the world
- smells like roses and exotic fruits
- abundance of flavour and richness
- appealing to lovers of big, bold wines
- wonderfully exuberant
- is grown in New Zealand, Washington State, Oregon, California and Australia
- pairs with spicy and boldly flavored dishes such as Chinese, Indian, Thai cuisines

Pinot Blanc
- full-bodied, rich white wine
- is well-known and esteemed

- brilliantly crisp in flavour
- refreshing
- is grown in France, Austria and Germany
- classic wine
- widely used for wine production
- is used extraordinarily well
- it is usually a blend to create a wonderfully opulent dessert wine
- pairs with Japanese cuisine, fish/seafood, salads

Pinot Gris (also called Pinot Grigio)
- two names for the same grape variety; first French, second Italian
- is light and pleasantly acidic
- is affordable and much-sought-after white wine
- is a mutation of Pinot Noir
- subtle and slightly perfumed
- is a wonderful wine
- is grown in Germany, Moravia, Romania, Slovenia, and Hungary
- also grown in California, Oregon, and New Zealand with excellent results
- pairs with breads, salads, soups, sauces, pastas, fish/seafood, pork, poultry

Riesling
- most famous grape variety in Germany
- produces wine that ranges from dry to extremely sweet
- alcohol level in German Riesling is reliably low
- made all over the world but famous and best grown in Germany
- a variety of styles
- sweet and expensive like dessert wines
- considered some of the best sweet wines in the world
- pairs with soup, fish/seafood, dairy, desserts, fruit/nuts, poultry, pork

Sauvignon Blanc
- one of the two grape varieties blended to produce the famous
- white wines of Bordeaux the other grape variety is Semillon
- grape variety is reliably fantastic
- great for the casual wine drinker
- Semillon best known as a popular wine
- produced in France, Chile, New Zealand and Australia
- when aged, becomes additionally full-bodied and opulent

- Semillon blended with Sauvignon Blanc makes a drier white wine
- pairs with ethnic dishes like Chinese, Indian and Thai cuisines

Rhone & Blended Wines
- region of France is more well-known for red wines than whites
- exciting and delicious
- unique in the world of wine
- Condrieu is the most famous and respected white wine
- floral and redolent of apricots
- enjoyed when it is young
- Grenache Blanc is a lovely white wine
- produces a sparkling white wine that is excellent
- the region's most famous for their dessert wine
- pairs with Chinese cuisine, fish/seafood, poultry

Rosé, Sparkling and Champagne
- traditionally comes from France and Spain
- briskly acidic
- the rose colour is made by crushing red grapes and allowing
- their skins to remain in contact with the juice for a few hours
- or days; this turns the juice any colour from pink to copper
- a freshness that most red wines do not have
- a weight that most white wines lack
- real rosé is wonderful
- wine with bubbles
- Champagne is the most famous sparkling wine
- from the Champagne region of France
- made from specific grapes
- produced according to a very strict method
- pairs with poultry, fish/seafood, summer type foods

RED WINES
Shiraz/Syrah
- grown mostly in California but also in France and Australia
- Shiraz grape was once thought to have originated in Persia
- a heavy red wine
- its spicy with peppery flavours

- such flavours are blackberry, plum, some licorice, and mocha
- rich and full
- should be served in a large bowl glass
- at a room temperature of 64°F – the warmest a red wine can be served
- Beef and hearty foods
- pairs with all spicy foods, Asian, Mexican cuisine

Beaujolais

- originally produced in the Beaujolais region of France
- distinct wine making process
- sugar is added to boost the alcohol content
- it barely qualifies as a wine
- most Beaujolais should be drunk within two years of being bottled
- vintage up to 10 years
- light, fruity and easy to drink
- aromas of pear and banana
- pairs with poultry, pork, red sauce pasta, strong cheeses

Pinot Noir

- light red wine
- some experts consider this wine to be the finest in the world
- originally grown in France but now in California, Oregon, Australia, and New Zealand
- the grape is extremely difficult to grow
- has a range of colours from a cherry red to brown
- flavours of earth, vanilla, oak-infused with fruity flavours like raspberry, strawberry, and plum
- pairs with beef, pork, strong cheeses, red sauce pasta, goose, wild game

Merlot

- name of the grape
- grown in France, California, and Chile
- not well suited for long aging
- mellow in complexity
- an easy drinking wine
- flavours of black cherry, plum, orange, and violets
- excellent complement to chocolate
- pairs with beef, hearty dishes, strong cheeses, chicken, red sauce, pasta

Cabernet Sauvignon

- name of the grape
- one of the world's most famous wines
- has a depth of complexity and a richness of flavour
- South America, Australia, Lebanon, California, Canada, and France
- mellow, hearty, mild and yet has a richness of flavour
- primary taste of black currant with overtones of blackberry
- and mint
- traditionally aged in oak so it takes on an oak vanilla-like flavour as well
- served in a large glass bowl
- pairs with beef, lamb, goose, cheeses, red sauce pasta, chocolate

Red Zinfandel

- originated in Italy is currently primarily grown in California
- grown on coast lines
- colour ranges from deep red to bordering black
- spicy and peppery with a hint of fruity flavours of berries
- narrow mouth glass
- served between room temperature and chilled
- can be served within a year or two
- when aged, the flavour is quite mellow
- red skins color the wine red (without it becomes a white)
- pairs with fast food, beef, strong cheeses

PORT

- Port originates from the Porto area, in the Douro Valley of Portugal
- Port first became popular when the English were at war with France
- "Port" can only refer to these wines one of the more famous of the fortified wines
- there are 48 authorized grape varieties which can go into a port
- pairs with strong cheese, fruit, and chocolate

Note: When pairing a wine with a Soup just remember the texture of the broth and the heartiness of the ingredients, the heartier or creamy the soup you pair with the same type of texture of wine.

FARE ISSENSUAL

Let's talk about food and sex; there's no getting away from the fact that these two basic human needs food and sex are sensually related. Scientists have said everything is ingrained in our brains, and both produce the same hormones dopamine and norepinephrine, which make us feel good.

I relate food and sex differently to sensual dining. The preparation and the experience are different; eating is like sex it's fulfilling a need, but sensual dining is the want of love and being a part of an intimate experience.

For instance; when someone has decided to have a romantic dinner, their shopping experience is an involved and detailed consumption of time and detail. When grocery shopping, it's about purchasing food to store and prepare when hungry. Another example is eating out; if you're hungry, the closest restaurant is the way to go or maybe a home order. When impressing that special someone you love and want to reflect your feelings; you will search and find create a sensual ambiance.

I was in the dating scene for several years, and this was proven to me repeatedly. When we were meeting for the first time and decided to eat something, it was the closest restaurant nearby. But if a first date, then my date would always take me to an intimate restaurant. The same if I was interested in the gentleman, I was dating then I would invite him for a homemade dinner. I would spend my whole day planning around an intimate sensual dinner at home.

Now, I'm not saying you will eat all your food most women will only consume a small amount. Let's not forget dessert because it promotes desire, especially if you share the dessert. Hey but just a heads up for the ladies be careful we tend once in a relationship we get comfortable and tend to eat more and exercise less!

Most sensuous foods are cold in temperature, creamy in texture and high in zinc. Fare does play a considerable part in romance; not only by setting the mood but also by making the sexual act more erotic and satisfying.

Food and sex have been acknowledging their partnership since as far back as Adam and Eve and the forbidden apple! Food can be very sensual and set up a romantic ambiance.

Cleopatra fed grapes to her lovers while lounging, and the great Casanova fed oysters to his women while they bathed. Radishes were considered a seductive food in Ancient Egypt while sweet potatoes in the Elizabethan Era. Ginseng, chilli peppers, and garlic are notorious stimulants and have been for many eras. Since time immemorial, food is to sex what romance is to sensuality.

Research has shown that certain smells or scents can arouse both sexes. For instance; women are supposedly aroused by the scent of cucumber, vanilla, musk, and banana bread. Men are stimulated by the smell of pump kin pie, cinnamon, vanilla, and lavender. Did you know that chocolate releases sexual hormones both in men and women? **BRING ON THE CHOCOLATE!**

Here are various food suggestions:

apples	artichokes
asparagus	bananas
beef wellington	body jams
bouillabaisse	breads
cheese	brochettes
cupcakes	candy
caviar	cheesecake
cherries	chicken
chocolate	cookies
cornish game hen	cream puffs
crepe suzette	cucumber
duck a l'orange	eggs benedict
escargot	exotic salads
filet mignon	flambés
fondues	fruit salad
glazed carrots	grapes
green beans	palm hearts
honey	ice cream
lobster	melon
mousse	mussels
nuts	raw oysters
pasta	pastries
pate	pineapple
figs	prawns
prosciutto	pumpkin pie
rack of lamb	raspberries
rice pilaf	salmon wellington
shish kabobs	soufflés
strawberries	stuffed potatoes
sushi	tortes
truffles	waffles
watermelon	whipping cream

TABLE SETTING FOR HOME DINING

The presentation also plays a factor when you use food for romantic purposes. The two have always appeared to connect in an intimate dance of the senses.

2 Dinner Plates
2 Salad Plates
2 Dinner Knives
2 Salad Forks
2 Soup Spoons
2 Dessert Spoons
2 Wine Glasses
1 Tablecloth or

2 Bread & Butter Plates
2 Cups and Saucers
2 Dinner Forks
2 Teaspoons
2 Dessert Forks
2 Water Glasses
2 Linen Napkins
2 Placemats

Setting Your Table for Dining:

- Place a placemat in front of each chair
- Place a service (dinner) plate on each placemat
- Left of the service plate, starting closest to the plate, place the dinner fork and the salad fork
- The right of the service plate, starting closest to the plate, put the dinner knife, the soup spoon, and the teaspoon
- Top of the service plate, position dessert fork or spoon or the appetizer fork, one pointing to the left and the other to the right
- Upper left of the service plate, place the bread & butter plate with the butter knife set on the plate
- The top right side of the service plate, place the cup and saucer
- Slightly right of center just above the cup and saucer, put the white wine glass
- Slightly left and above the white wine glass, place the red wine glass
- Slightly left and above the red wine glass place the water glass. The Soup Bowl or Salad Plate are set on top of the service plate. Fold the napkin and put under the fork area

TABLE CENTERPIECE

A few simple skills to produce beautiful table arrangements consistently; start with these tips for all your dinner table arrangements:

- An arrangement that looks good from all sides of the dinner table for your guests to admire.
- An arrangement should be about five inches or lower; so, guests can easily see over it.
- Don't put highly scented flowers on the dinner table because their aroma can complete with the food aromas and a guest may be allergic to the strong scent as well.
- White taper candles are dramatic; tea candles are more subtle yet both lovely.

Country: Arrange an assortment of loaves of bread in the center of your table and cut out the center of the loaves and put a tea candle in each cutout, sprinkle a mixture of dried fruits and nuts around them.

Sophisticated: All white linen with white flowers and baby's breath, with touches of gold or silver along with candelabra's or wine glasses, turn upside down with candles sitting on the foot of the glass, and a flower inside the bowl.

Dramatic: Colour is the focus of this theme; deep tones even black. Use chiffon and wrap around vases containing colour water of contrast with floating candles drape the chiffon down the opposite sides of your table ---- napkins placed in the wine glasses.

Garden: Have several jars and put in a variety of herbs like dill, rosemary, mint, basil, thyme, lavender, and flowering herbs, sits in a high-sided bowl; a smaller bowl within keeps the stems in place. Use earth colours in accessories.

Simplistic: A sizeable full vase with a variety of limes, lemons and mandarin oranges with a variety of sizes of candles with pastel colours of the fruit.

Theme: Halloween, Thanksgiving, Girls Night, Birthday's or Midnight in Paris it's just how much time and effort you want to put into it.

The world of imagination is at the dawn of your thoughts, have fun and enjoy the artistic realm that your guests will be at awe. Remember art is in the eye of the beholder.

DINING AMBIANCE

2	Roses of Petals
28	Tea-light Candles
1	Tall Vase
1	Rose with Greenery
1	White Placemat

Soft Room Lighting
Fireplace (if you have one)
Romantic Mood Music

- • Place white placemat at the center of the table
- • Place the 28 tea-light candles to form a heart shape
- • Place the vase with rose and greenery in the center
- • Sprinkle the rose petals around the outside of the heart
- • Colour of the rose and rose petals would be your choice
- • Recommended colour is either red or her favourite color
- • No overhead lighting unless you have a dimmer
- • Living room lighting should be soft
- • Fireplace ignited or put on
- • Place other tea-light candles in holders around the room
- • Romantic mood music playing in the background
- • Duration of music playlist should be at least 3 to 4 hours

Dinner music is one of your best tools for creating the ambiance for your guest or significant other. Dinner party music shouldn't bother your guests. I received a bit of an education on this point recently when a dinner guest asked (very politely) if I could change the jazz music I had on. She said that she found the unresolved tension of the jazz chords distracting. When I listened for a few minutes, I realized she had a point. I may love the music, but it was drawing attention to itself. I was wrong to assume that it worked well for a dinner party.

Soft classical music is always the right choice if in doubt. If you choose music with singing, be careful to keep it low enough that people aren't trying to listen to the words instead of each other. Choosing your dinner music is something you can do well in advance. Music is the core of creating an ambiance for your guests. They are some things you should keep in mind while setting the ambiance for your dining pleasure:

- Match your music selection to fit the theme of the evening.
- Your playlist should be the length of the evening.

- Keep it self-motivated with a variety of tunes to suit the ambiance you want your guests to experience.
- Alter your music based on the time of day that you're dining. For instance; breakfast tranquil, brunch or lunch a little more elevated, happy hour should be energetic, and dinner a mix of vibrant, subtle and adoring.
- Don't play the music too loud; you don't want the music to compete with your guest's conversation.

When having a dinner party, I'm more partial to instrumentals than vocals, although once again variety is the spice of life. Here are some selections to set the theme of your dinner party:

- Romantic; Love songs, R & B & Soul
- Bistro; Jazz, Blues even some Folk
- Elegant Dining; French, Latin, and Classical
- Family Style; Easy Listening, a nice variety
- Barbeque; Caribbean influence, Country, and Rock
- Cocktail; Instrumentals of different era's

A FARE CHANCE

VANITY
FARE

A FARE CHANCE

Category: Appetizer
Servings: 5 to 7 guests
Prep Time: 20-25 minutes
Cooking Time: 10 minutes
Serve with: White Wine

AWE SHUCKS I LOVE YOU
(Oyster Pico de Gallo)

10 Large	Oysters (cut in half)
2 Large	Roma Tomatoes (seeded and chopped)
1 Cup	Red Onion (finely chopped)
1 Large	Jalapeno (seeded and chopped)
½ Cup	Cilantro (finely chopped)
2 Large	Limes (juice)
1 Large	Egg (beaten)
2 Cups	Flour
4 Cups	Vegetable or Canola Oil
½ Cup	Monterey Jack Cheese (shredded)
20 Mini	Taco Cups
Pinch	Seasoning Salt

Sauce:

3 Tbsp.	Honey
1/4 Cup	Cilantro (finely chopped)
1 Cup	Mayonnaise
1 Large	Lime (Juice)

Sauce ingredients into a blender and blend at high speed for 2 minutes

1. Toss the chopped tomatoes, red onion, jalapeno, ¼ cup cilantro together in a bowl with the juice of 1 lime and a pinch of salt and pepper
2. Coat oysters in egg mixture then coat with flour
3. Heat oil to frying temperature (use a couple of corn kernels once they pop the oil is ready)
4. Deep fry oysters in oil and remove once golden crisp then place on paper towel to drain excess oil and sprinkle with seasoning salt
5. Drain excess liquid from salsa
6. To prepare; fill mini taco cups with ½ tsp. of salsa, then oyster, sprinkle cheese on oyster then top with sauce and serve immediately

Category: Appetizer
Servings: 2 to 4 guests
Prep Time: 10 minutes
Cooking Time: 20 to 30 minutes
Serve with: Soya sauce to dip

LET'S DO PICNIC IN THE PORK
(Pork Bites)

1 Pound	Boneless Pork Cubes
1 Large	Egg (whisked)
3 Tbsps.	Soya Sauce
4 Cups	Canola/Vegetable Oil
2 Cups	Flour
1 Tbsp.	Granulated Garlic
2 Tbsps.	Seasoning Salt

1. Add soya and garlic to egg mix then add pork to egg mixture and coat
2. Fill Ziploc bag with flour
3. Add pork to bag of flour
4. Shake to coat pork
5. Shake excess flour off pork then add to oil and deep fry
6. Place on paper towel, season with seasoning salt, granulated garlic
7. Place on roasting pan
8. Bake in preheated 350° oven for 20 minutes

*Want to know when your oil is ready for deep frying add 4 corn cornels into Oil, when all of them pop, remove and start deep frying.

Category: Appetizer
Servings: 2 to 4 guests
Prep Time: 4 hours
Cooking Time: 3-4 minutes
Serve with: Wasabi Aioli

STEAK WITH ME SWEET MIRIN

(Beef Shish kabob)

2 Pound	Sirloin Steak
1 Cup	Vegetable Oil
½ Cup	Sake
¼ Cup	Sweet Mirin Seasoning Liquid
1 Cup	Soya Sauce
1 Cup	Cilantro (chopped finely)
1 Cup	Parsley (chopped finely)
4 Large	Green Onions (Diced)
½ Cup	Ginger (Grated finely)
½ Cup	Garlic (chopped finely)
8	Skewer Sticks

1. Cut steak into 24 cubes
2. Combine all ingredients in a large Ziploc plastic bag
3. Add cubed steak to bag of marinade
4. Refrigerator for 4 hours
5. Remove steak cubes from bag and discard marinade
6. Put 3 cubes on each skewer
7. Grill 3 minutes on each side or until desired doneness

WASABI AIOLI

½ Cup Mayonnaise
2 Tsp. Wasabi Paste
2 Tsp. Lemon Juice
1 Tsp. Granulated Garlic

Combine all Aioli ingredients and blend then serve as a kabob dip.

Category: Appetizer
Servings: 2 to 4 guests
Prep Time: 5-6 Hours
Cooking Time: N/A
Serve: Endive leaves

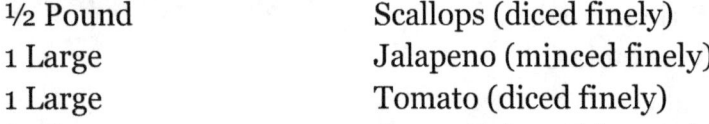

CRUDO'S TO US
(Scallop Ceviche)

½ Pound	Scallops (diced finely)
1 Large	Jalapeno (minced finely)
1 Large	Tomato (diced finely)
¼ Cup	Green Onions (chopped finely)
¼ Cup	Celery (diced finely)
Juice	6 Limes
Juice	1 Lemon
1 Medium	Avocado (diced)
¼ Cup	Cilantro (chopped finely)
4 Large	Endives

1. Prepare all above ingredients as instructed above
2. Put all ingredients other than avocado in a bowl and toss
3. Refrigerate and let marinade for 4 hours
4. Tossing the ceviche every ½ hour
5. Break up Endives into individual leaves
6. Wash and pat dry individually
7. After 4 hours make sure the Scallops are opaque (solid white)
8. Now add Avocado and toss
9. Place the ceviche in a serving bowl with tablespoon surrounded by endive
10. Or you can put a tablespoon of Ceviche on each

Category: Appetizer
Servings: 4 to 6 guests
Prep Time: 15 to 20 minutes
Cooking Time: N/A
Served with: Crostini or Crackers

DON'T BE BLEU WE CAN STILL BRIE FRIENDS
(Cheese Ball)

1 Cup	Crème Cheese
1 Cup	Blue Cheese (crumbled)
1 Cup	Smoked Cheese (shredded)
1 Cup	Brie Cheese (diced)
4 Tbsps.	Worcestershire Sauce
¼ Cup	Parsley (minced)
2 Tbsps.	Dry Garlic (minced)
3 Tbsps.	Dry Onion (minced)
1 Cup	Mayonnaise
1 Cup	Sunflower Seeds (roasted)

1. Except the parsley and seeds mix all ingredients in bowl
2. Refrigerate for 1 hour
3. Roast the seeds at 350° until they turn golden then cool
4. Form cheese mixture into a ball
5. Before serving sprinkle with parsley and seeds all over the ball
6. Keep refrigerated until serving

Category: Appetizer
Servings: 3 to 4 guests
Prep Time: 15-20 minutes
Cooking Time: 10 to 15 minutes
Served with: White Wine

YOU MUSHROOM MY INSPIRATION
(Stuffed Mushrooms)

12 Medium	Mushrooms (wash and pat dry)
1 Cup	Bacon (finely chopped)
1 Pkg.	Cream Cheese (250 g room temp)
¼ Cup	Onion (chopped finely)
1 Tbsp.	Garlic (chopped finely)
1 Tbsp.	Parsley (dry flakes)
3 Tbsps.	Worcestershire Sauce
½ Cup	Parmesan shavings
2 Tbsps.	Butter (melted)

1. Soften crème cheese at room temperature
2. Remove stem from mushrooms and set aside
3. Wash and pat dry each mushroom
4. Place mushroom caps on cookie sheet
5. Fry bacon, cool chopped finely, and set aside
6. Diced mushroom stems finely
7. Melt butter then add mushroom stems, onion and garlic toss until tender
8. Combine mushroom mixture, Worcestershire, parsley and bacon to crème cheese
9. Mix all ingredients except Parmesan cheese
10. Fill mushroom caps with cheese mixture
11. Top each filled cap with 2-3 shavings of Parmesan cheese
12. 10. Bake in 375° preheated oven 10 to 15 minutes or until bubbling

Category: Appetizer
Servings: 6 to 8 guests
Prep Time: 15 minutes
Cooking Time: N/A
Serve with: Sake or White Wine

WASA AND SASHI ARE SOYA HAPPY

(Salmon & Cucumber)

2 Cups	Salmon Sashimi (finely diced)
1 Cup	Green Onions (finely diced)
1 Stalk	Celery (finely diced)
2 Tbsps.	Sesame Seeds (roasted)
¼ Cup	Lime Juice
2 Tbsps.	Soya Sauce
3 Tbsps.	Sake
2 Tbsps.	Sesame Seed Oil
1 Tsp.	Wasabi Paste
2 Large	Avocado (finely mashed)
1 Large	English Cucumber (sliced ½ inch thick)

1. Mix the first eight ingredients together then refrigerate for 2 hours
2. Peel, scoop and mash avocado add wasabi and mix into a creamy spread
3. Wash skin of cucumber and pat dry
4. Slice cucumber into ½ inch thickness and discard ends
5. Spread a teaspoon of avocado mixture on cucumber slice
6. Add heaping teaspoon of salmon mixture on top of avocado spread
7. Serve immediately or refrigerate for not more than hour then serve

Category: Appetizer
Servings: 4 to 6 guests
Prep Time: 15 minutes
Cooking Time: 5 minutes
Serve with: Sake or White Wine

LET'S SCALLOP INTO THE SUNSET

(Seared Scallops)

12 Large	Scallops
12 Large	Wonton Spoons
3 Tbsps.	Butter (melted)
1 Large	Lemon (juice)
1 Cup	White Wine
1 Tsp.	Granulated Garlic
½ Tsp.	Seasoning Salt
2 Tbsps.	Parsley (dry)

1. Place wonton spoons on a large platter
2. Melt Butter in sauté pan
3. Seared Scallops in a 12 to 14-inch sauté pan on high heat for 1 minutes
4. Make sure the scallops don't touch each other
5. Once seared add the rest of the ingredients and lower heat to medium
6. Let sit for 2 to 3 minutes
7. Place a scallop on each wonton spoon
8. Drizzle ½ teaspoon of sauce over each scallop
9. Serve immediately

Category: Appetizer
Servings: 8 to 10 guests
Prep Time: 20 minutes
Cooking Time: N/A
Serve with: Rose or White Wine

SALMON ELSE LOVES HER LOXS
(Checkerboard)

1 Pkg.	Pumpernickel Bread (square shape)
1 Pkg.	Salmon Lox
2 Jars	Black Caviar or Roe (any type)
1 Small	Red Onion (finely diced)
2 Large	Eggs (devilled)
1 250 ml	Soft Cream Cheese

1. Line up squares as if a checkerboard 6 per line across and 6 per line down which should be 36 squares on square platter
2. 18 squares should be for caviar and 18 squares for salmon lox
3. Mix Cream Cheese, devilled egg, and red onion together
4. Spread cream cheese mixture on each bread square
5. Spread ½ teaspoon caviar on each of the 18 squares
6. Cut lox into same size squares as the bread and place on bread
7. Place squares in checkerboard fashion on platter
8. Cover and refrigerate until serving

Category: Appetizer
Servings: 2 to 4 guests
Prep Time: 8 minutes
Cooking Time: N/A
Served with: Crostini's or Crackers

DON'T BE CRABBY SPREAD THE LOVE
(Cajun Crab Spread)

½ Cup	Crab (finely chopped)
1 Cup	Crème Cheese
¼ Cup	Mayonnaise
½ Tsp.	Worcestershire Sauce
½ Tsp.	Seasoning Salt
1 Tbsp.	Pimentos (finely chopped)
½ Tsp.	Cayenne Pepper
½ Tsp.	Granulated Garlic
½ Tsp.	Parsley (dry)

1. Chop Crab and Pimentos
2. Mix all the above ingredients in a bowl
3. Refrigerate for 2 hours
4. Then Serve

Category: Appetizer
Servings: 4 to 6 guests
Prep Time: 10-15 minutes
Cooking Time: 20-30 minutes
Serve with: White Wine

YOU SPICE UP MY LIFE

(Stuffed Jalapeno Peppers)

12 Large	Jalapeno Peppers (half & cleaned)
½ Cup	Green Pepper (diced finely)
½ Cup	Red Pepper (diced finely)
1 Large	Green Onions (chopped finely)
1 250 ml	Cream Cheese
1 Cup	Mozzarella Cheese (shredded)
½ Cup	Bacon (chopped finely)
2 Tbsps.	Worcestershire Sauce
½ Tsp.	Cayenne Pepper

1. Preheat the oven to 375°.
2. Slice the jalapeños half lengthwise (like a boat shape)
3. Scrape out all the seeds and ribs from each jalapeño with a spoon
4. Cook the bacon and chop finely
5. Dice Green and Red Peppers
6. Chop green onions finely
7. Mix all ingredients in a bowl except jalapeños
8. Spoon & pack the filling into jalapeños
9. Arrange jalapeños on parchment paper lined baking sheet
10. Bake for 20-30 minutes, or until the cheese browning
11. Serve immediately

Category: Appetizer
Servings: 2 to 4 guests
Prep Time: 10 minutes
Cooking Time: 25 to 35 minutes
Serve with: Ranch or Bleu Cheese Dip

PUT A WING ON IT
(Hot Wings)

1 Pound	Chicken Wings
2 Cup	Hot Sauce
½ Cup	Barbeque Sauce
1 Tsp.	Onion (dry minced)
1 Tsp.	Garlic (dry minced)
1 Tsp.	Parsley (dry)
2 Tsp.	Seasoning Salt

1. Mix all ingredients (except chicken wings) in a bowl
2. Place wings into mixture and toss until coated
3. Arrange on a cookie sheet
4. Bake wings in 375° preheated oven for 25 to 35 minutes
5. Serve immediately

Category: Appetizer
Servings: 3 to 4 guests
Prep Time: 20 minutes
Cooking Time: 10 to 17 minutes
Serve with: Aioli or Cocktail Sauce

YOU ARE CRABULOUS
(Mini Crab Balls)

2 ½ Cups	Dungeness Crab
2 Cups	Mashed Potatoes
4 Large	Green Onions (chopped)
3 Cups	Breadcrumbs
2 Cups	Flour
½ Cup	Sour Cream
4 Large	Eggs
2 Tbsps.	Garlic Powder
2 Tbsps.	Parsley (dry)
To Taste	Seasoning Salt
3 Cups	Canola or Vegetable Oil

1. Combine crab, potatoes, onions, 1 cup of breadcrumbs, ½ cup of flour, sour cream, 2 eggs, garlic, and parsley in a bowl blend together
2. Form bite size balls and place on a plate
3. Pour the rest of the breadcrumbs on a plate
4. Pour the rest of the flour on another plate
5. Whisk 2 eggs in a bowl
6. Roll crab balls in flour
7. Dip crab balls in egg mixture
8. Roll crab balls in breadcrumbs
9. Heat oil to 350° place balls in hot oil until crispy golden on each side
10. Place on paper towel and season with seasoning salt and serve

Remember to put a popcorn kernel in the oil as it heats. The popcorn will pop when the oil is between 350°F and 365°F the perfect temperature for deep frying.

Category: Appetizer
Servings: 3 to 4 guests
Prep Time: 5 minutes
Cooking Time: 7-10 minutes
Serve with: White Wine

KEEP IT SHRIMPLE SWEETHEART

(Cajun Prawns)

16 Large	Prawns (de-shelled)
¼ Cup	Olive Oil
2 Tbsps.	Lemon Juice
1 Tbsp.	Cajun Spice
½ Tsp.	Paprika
1 Tsp.	Parsley (dry)
1 Tsp.	Granulated Garlic
1 Tsp.	Onion (dry minced)

1. Add all the above ingredients (except prawns) in a bowl and mix
2. Toss the prawns in mixture
3. Marinate Prawns in fridge ½ hour
4. Either put on skewers (4 to a skewer) or individually on a cookie sheet
5. Barbeque or bake in 350° preheated oven for 10 minutes or until pink

Soak skewer sticks in water for 30 minutes.

Category: Appetizer
Servings: 2 to 4 guests
Prep Time: 10 minutes
Cooking Time: 10 minutes
Serve with: French Bread

THINGS COULD GET STEAMY
(Wine Steamed Mussels)

3 Pounds	Mussels (cleaned & de-bearded)
1 Cup	Onion (chopped)
1 Cup	Tomato (diced)
1 Cup	White Wine
1 Cup	Chicken or Vegetable Broth
3 Tbsps.	Butter (melted)
2 Tbsps.	Parsley (dry minced)
1 Tbsp.	Garlic (minced)
2 Tbsps.	Worcestershire Sauce

1. De-beard Mussels and rinse
2. In a soup pot melt butter
3. Add onions, garlic and tomatoes
4. Cook until tender
5. Add wine, broth, parsley and Worcestershire to pot
6. Boil on high until steaming then add mussels
7. Cover for 7 to 10 minutes or until shells open
8. Pour liquid and mussels in a serving bowl
9. Serve immediately

To de-beard the mussels means to pull off the mini beard or what looks like a beard which is usually located at the end of the mussel.

Can use Clams in place of Mussels eliminating tomatoes.

Category: Appetizer
Servings: 4 to 6 guests
Prep Time: 20 minutes
Cooking Time: 15 to 20 minutes
Serve with: White Wine

Me:

YOU ARE MY TUNACORN
(Tuna Bake Bites)

2 Cans	Tuna (flaked)
2 Large	Eggs (hard boiled & finely chopped)
3 Large	Green Onions (finely chopped)
½ Cup	Green Pepper (finely chopped)
¼ Cup	Red Pepper (finely chopped)
1 Cup	Cheddar Cheese (grated)
½ Cup	Mozzarella Cheese (grated)
3 Tbsps.	Hamburger Relish
½ Cup	Mayonnaise
3 Tbsps.	Worcestershire Sauce
1 Tsp.	Garlic (dry minced)
1 Large	Baguette (sliced 1 inch thick)

1. Mix all the above together
2. Cut Baguette inch thick slices
3. Spoon 1 heaping tablespoon of tuna mixture on each slice
4. Place on cookie sheet
5. Bake for 15 to 20 minutes in 350° preheated oven until bubbling
6. Serve immediately

Category: Appetizer
Servings: 4 to 6 guests
Prep Time: 15 minutes
Cooking Time: 20 minutes
Serve with: Cocktail sauce

YOUR LOVE IS UNSHELLFISH
(Scallops wrapped in Bacon)

| 24 | Scallops (small) |
| 1 Pound | Bacon |

1. Cut bacon strips in half
2. Wrap bacon half around scallop
3. Place seam down on cookie sheet
4. Bake in 400° preheated oven until bacon is cooked
5. Serve with seafood sauce

SEAFOOD SAUCE

1 Cup	Ketchup
½ Cup	Horseradish
½ Cup	Worcestershire Sauce
¼ Cup	Chili Sauce
2 Tbsps.	Lemon Juice
2 Large	Green Onions (chopped)

Mix all above ingredients in bowl and serve.

Category: Appetizer
Servings: 6 to 8 guests
Prep Time: 45 minutes
Cooking Time: N/A
Serve with: Baguette (sliced)

OLIVE OF ME LOVES OLIVE OF YOU
(Pizza Salsa)

1 ½ Cups	Parmesan Cheese (grated)
½ cup	Parsley (chopped finely)
½ cup	Cilantro (chopped finely)
2 Large	Tomatoes (diced finely)
3 Large	Mushrooms (diced finely)
1 Can	Black Olives (diced finely)
1 Large	Green Pepper (diced finely)
2 Large	Garlic Cloves (minced)
1 Large	Red Onion (diced finely)
½ Cup	White Wine
1 Tsp.	Lemon Juice
1 Cup	Olive Oil
1/3 Cup	White Vinegar
2 Tbsps.	Seasoning Salt
1 Large	Baguette

1. In a large bowl combine all above ingredients
2. Cover and store in refrigerator overnight
3. Cut Baguette into inch thick slices
4. Scoop 1 to 2 tablespoons of mixture on each slice
5. Serve immediately

"Lettuce romaince our love spending thyme brock n' oli us."

A FARE CHANCE

FARE SHARE

A FARE CHANCE

Category: Soup
Servings: 4 to 6 guests
Prep Time: 25 minutes
Cooking Time: 2 hours
Serve with: Sliced Baguette

I'M TONGUE THAI OVER YOU

(Thai Prawn)

16 Large	Prawns (cut in half)
1 Can	Coconut Milk
5 Cups	Chicken Broth or Vegetable Broth
2 Tbsp.	Red Curry Paste
1 Tbsp.	Almond Butter
2 Tbsp.	Lime Juice
1 Tbsp.	Garlic (mince)
2 Cups	Carrots (slice)
1 Cup	Celery (chop)
1 Cup	Green Pepper (dice)
1 Cup	Onion (dice)
1 Tbsp.	Cilantro (mince)
1 Tbsp.	Basil (mince)
1 Tbsp.	Ginger (grate)
1 Tsp.	Chili Flakes
½ Tsp.	Curry Powder

1. Pour chicken broth into soup pot
2. Add vegetables
3. Bring to a boil
4. Turn down low to medium
5. Add rest of the ingredients, whisk then cover for 10 minutes
6. Add prawns and cook until pink
7. Serve immediately

Category: Dessert
Servings: 2 to 4 guests
Prep Time: 15 minutes
Cooking Time: 35 to 45 minutes
Serve with: Coffee or Dessert Wine

I'M APPLEY TO KNOW YOU SUGAR
(Apple Crisp)

6 Cups	Apples (peel, core & slice)
½ Cup	Brown Sugar
3 Tbsps.	Lemon Juice
½ Tbsp.	Cinnamon

Topping:

2 Cups	Flour
1 Cup	Brown Sugar
1 Tbsp.	Cinnamon
½ Cup	Butter

1. Toss apples with sugar, juice and cinnamon
2. Place in slightly greased 9 x 11 baking dish
3. Mix flour, sugar, cinnamon and butter well
4. Sprinkle topping over apples
5. Place in 350 ° preheated oven for about 35 to 45 minutes or until tender
6. 6Serve with whipped cream or cool whip

Any apple is good except Mac's also try peaches or pears

FARE SHARE

Category: Soup
Servings: 4 to 6 guests
Prep Time: 15 minutes
Cooking Time: 35 to 60 minutes
Serve with: Garlic Bread

I KNEW YOU WOULD BE TRUFFLE
(Lobster Chowder)

1 Pound	Lobster Meat (chop)
12 Large	Prawns (cut in half)
12 Small	Scallops
5 Large	Potatoes (cube)
2 Large	Carrot (slice)
1 Large	Onion (dice)
1 Cup	Celery (chop)
1 Cup	Green Pepper (chop)
1 Cup	Red Pepper (chop)
¼ Cup	Butter
1 Can	Consommé Soup
2 Cups	Chicken Broth
2 Cups	Tomato Soup
2 Cups	Cream
1 Cup	White Wine
2 Large	Bay Leaf's
1 Tbsp.	Thyme
2 Tsps.	Pepper
3 Tbsps.	Truffle Oil

1. Melt butter, add onions and cook until tender
2. Except seafood, cream and oil add rest of ingredients to onions
3. When vegetables are tender add cream, oil and seafood
4. Let simmer for 1 hour
5. Serve with bread

Category: Dessert
Servings: 2 to 4 guests
Prep Time: 15 minutes
Cooking Time: 10 minutes
Serve with: Coffee, Tea or Dessert Wine

I APPEACHIATE YOU BABY
(Peaches & Ice Cream)

1 Can	Peaches
½ Cup	Grand Marnier
1 Tsp.	Cinnamon
½ Cup	Almonds (chopped & roasted)
½ Cup	Water (cold)
1 Tsp.	Cornstarch
6-8 Scoops	Ice Cream (Vanilla)

1. Layer almonds on a cookie sheet then sprinkle with cinnamon
2. Roast sliced almonds 400° preheated oven until golden
3. Set almonds aside to cool
4. Pour peaches and juice in pot and bring to a boil
5. Turn down to medium heat
6. Add Grand Marnier and stir
7. Add 1 Tsp. of cornstarch to ½ cup of water and stir
8. Add cornstarch mixture to pot of peaches
9. Whisk until mixture bubbles and thickens then remove from heat
10. Put 2 scoops of ice cream in each dish or bowl
11. Pour ½ cup of peach mixture over ice cream
12. Sprinkle the roasted almonds
13. Serve immediately

Category: Soup
Servings: 4 to 6 guests
Prep Time: 20 minutes
Cooking Time: 1 to ½ hours
Serve with: White Wine

TO MY DEAREST CLOVE
(French Onion)

3 Large	Onions (slice)
1 Tbsp.	Garlic (mince)
1 Cup	Mozzarella Cheese (slice)
1 Cup	Swiss (grate)
1 Cup	Parmesan (shave)
4 Slices	Baguette (slice & toasted)
2 Tbsps.	Butter
2 Cans	Campbell's Onion Soup
1 Cup	White Wine
4 Cups	Chicken Broth
2 Large	Bay Leaf
1 Tsp.	Thyme

1. Mix all the cheeses together and put aside
2. Cook onions in butter until tender
3. Add the rest of ingredients except cheese and bread
4. Bring to a boil then cover and simmer for 1 hour
5. Add third of the cheese to soup bowl
6. Add a slice of toasted bread into each bowl
7. Pour soup into bowls
8. Cover the soup with the rest of the cheese
9. Place under broiler until cheese is bubbling
10. Serve immediately

Soup bowls should be able to be place under a broiler

Category: Dessert
Servings: 6 to 8 guests
Prep Time: 10 minutes
Cooking Time: 15 to 18 minutes
Serve with: Coffee or Dessert Wine

YOU'RE A FINE COOKIE

(Gluten Free Almond Cookies)

2 Cups	Blanche Almonds
1 Cup	Icing Sugar
3 Large	Egg Whites
1/2 Tbsp.	Almond Extract

1. Food process almonds and sugar until almond fine in consistency
2. Add egg whites and extract process until a firm paste
3. Refrigerate for 10 to 15 minutes
4. 1 teaspoon of mixture in hand roll into a ball
5. Place on non-stick cookie sheet
6. Gently press each cookie a little flat on cookie sheet
7. Bake in preheated 325° oven for 18 minutes or until lightly browned
8. Cool on a rack or racks
9. Store in an airtight container for about a week
10. Makes between 18 to 24 cookies

Category: Soup
Servings: 6 to 8 guests
Prep Time: 25 minutes
Cooking Time: 1 hour
Serve with: Sliced French Bread

LEEKS REVEAL YOU'RE A SPUD

(Vichyssoise)

10 Large	Potatoes (slice)
2 Large	Leeks (slice)
1 Large	Onion (dice)
4 Large	Mushrooms (slice thinly)
8 Slices	Bacon (crumble)
3 Tbsps.	Butter (melt)
4 Cups	Cream
3 Cans	Consommé
2 Cups	Chicken Broth
1 Cup	White Wine
2 Large	Bay Leaf
1 Tbsp.	Thyme
2 Tbsps.	Parsley
1 Tbsp.	Seasoning Salt
1 Tbsp.	Pepper

1. Separate the green part from the white part of the leek
2. Wash each green leaf thoroughly
3. Layered green leaves on top of each other
4. Slice horizontally
5. Slice in half the white part of the leek and wash
6. Take each half and slice horizontally
7. Melt butter in soup pot
8. Add leeks and onion into butter cook until tender
9. Cook bacon crisp, crumble and add to leek mixture
10. Except for cream add the rest of the ingredients and cook on medium
11. Turning the broth every 10 minutes until potatoes are tender
12. When potatoes tender, mash potatoes in soup mixture
13. Stir in cream simmer for 30 minutes covered stirring every 10 minutes
14. Turn off soup and let sit 5 minutes before serving

Category: Dessert
Servings: 6 to 8 guests
Prep Time: 15 minutes
Cooking Time: 15 minutes
Serve with: Coffee, Tea or Dessert Wine

I'M SWEET OVER YOU PUDDIN
(Cake & Pudding)

1	Angel Food Cake (store bought)
1 Large	Pistachio Pudding
1 Large	Cool Whip (thaw)
1 Cup	Pistachio Nuts (finely chopped)
12	Maraschino Cherries (halves)

1. Place cake on a plate that is 3 times larger
2. Prepare pudding to package instructions
3. Combine pudding, cool whip fold until fully blended
4. Pour over cake until completely covered
5. Sprinkle the pistachio nuts over cake
6. Place cherries around the top of the cake
7. Refrigerate for 1 hour then cut and serve

Category: Soup
Servings: 3 to 4 guests
Prep Time: 20 minutes
Cooking Time: 45 minutes
Serve with: Garlic Bread

I YAM WANTING YOU

(Yam & Carrot)

1 Large	Yam (peel and quarter)
4 Large	Carrots (peel and chop)
½ Large	Onion (quarter)
¼ Tsp.	Red Chili Flakes
¼ Tsp.	Cinnamon (ground)
½ Tsp.	Cayenne Pepper
½ Tsp.	Thyme
1 Cup	Coconut Milk
1 Large	Lime (juice)
6 Cups	Chicken Broth or Vegetable Broth
To Taste	Salt & Pepper

1. Add all ingredients to large soup pot
2. Bring to a boil
3. Turn to medium to low until vegetables are tender
4. Turn off element uncover and let stand to cool
5. Pour 3 cups at a time in blender then blend until creamy
6. Pour creamy soup back into the pot cover on low heat for 30 minutes
7. Stir every 10 minutes
8. Serve with bread

Category: Dessert
Servings: 4 to 6 guests
Prep Time: 15 minutes
Cooking Time: 1 ½ hours
Serve with: Milk, Coffee, Tea or Dessert Wine

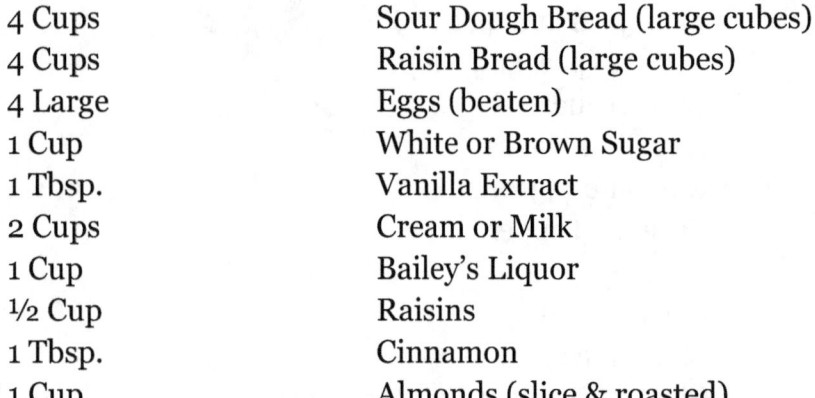

THANKS FOR PUDDING ME FIRST
(Bread Pudding)

4 Cups	Sour Dough Bread (large cubes)
4 Cups	Raisin Bread (large cubes)
4 Large	Eggs (beaten)
1 Cup	White or Brown Sugar
1 Tbsp.	Vanilla Extract
2 Cups	Cream or Milk
1 Cup	Bailey's Liquor
½ Cup	Raisins
1 Tbsp.	Cinnamon
1 Cup	Almonds (slice & roasted)

1. Roast almonds for 5 minutes in 425° preheated oven on cookie sheet
2. Set almonds aside
3. Mix all the above ingredients in a bowl
4. Pour mixture into a lightly butter shallow 9 x 13 baking dish
5. Sprinkle with roasted almonds
6. Submerge baking dish in another pan filled with an inch of boiling water
7. Bake 350° preheated oven for 1 hour
8. Doneness can be checked by putting a knife through the center and if the knife comes out clear it's done
9. Let the pudding set for 15 minutes before serving

Children can have this because the alcohol burns off in the baking

Category: Soup
Servings: 2 to 4 guests
Prep Time: 20 minutes
Cooking Time: 1 hour
Serve with: French Bread

PEAS BE MY CHICKY-BOO

(Chick-Pea)

2 Cans	Chickpeas (15.5 ounces each & rinse)
1 Large	Onion (dice)
2 Large	Potato (dice)
1 Tbsp.	Garlic (mince)
6 Cups	Chicken Broth or Vegetable Stock
1 Cup	Cream
1 Tbsp.	Parsley (dry)
To Taste	Salt & Pepper

1. Except for cream & parsley add all ingredients to soup pot
2. Bring to a boil then turn to low and cover for 30 minutes
3. When vegetables are tender, turn off element, uncover and let stand
4. Once cool put 3 cups at a time in a blender and blend until creamy
5. Pour creamy soup back into the pot, cover and set on low heat
6. Add cream, parsley, salt and pepper and stir
7. Heat covered on medium to low heat for 10 minutes then serve

Category: Dessert
Servings: 4 to 6 guests
Prep Time: 15 minutes
Cooking Time: ½ hour
Serve with: Coffee, Tea or Dessert Wine

YOU MAKE MY LIFE PEARFECT
(Pear & Pudding Pie)

1 Large	Pie Shell (store bought)
2 Cans	Half Pears (15 ounce each)
4 Cups	Custard (store bought-pre-made)
1 Cup	Brown Sugar
1 Tbsp.	Cinnamon
1 Cup	Almonds (crumble)
1 Cup	Unsalted Cold Butter
1 Cup	All-purpose Flour or Almond Flour

Pie

1. Preheat oven at 350 degrees
2. Pre-cook pie crust until golden and cool
3. Add custard to pie shell halfway up
4. Drain Pears and place on top of custard face down
5. Top with crumble topping
6. Bake 350° preheated oven for 30 minutes
7. Set aside until cool then serve

Crumble Topping

1. Grate cold butter into a large bowl
2. Add sugar, flour, cinnamon, almonds
3. Work the butter into the mixture
4. Until the mixture forms coarse crumbs
5. Sprinkle over pears

Category: Soup
Servings: 2 to 4 guests
Prep Time: 10 minutes
Cooking Time: 1 to 1 ½ hours
Serve with: French Bread

YOU'RE SOUPER HOT

(Asian Chicken)

2	Chicken Breasts (cube)
3 Large	Carrots (slice)
1 Large	Onion (dice)
3 Sticks	Celery (dice)
12 Small	Mushrooms (quarter)
4 Small	Bok Choy (chop)
4 Cups	Chicken Broth
1 Tbsp.	Seasoning Salt
3 Tbsps.	Granulated Garlic
1 Tbsp.	Pepper
3 Cups	Cauliflower Rice

1. Except rice put all the above ingredients in soup pot
2. Bring to a boil, cover and turn down to medium to low heat for 1 hour
3. Cook rice to package instructions
4. Add rice to broth and stir
5. Serve with bread

Category: Dessert
Servings: 2 to 4 guests
Prep Time: 25 minutes
Time to Set: 3 hours
Serve with: Coffee, Tea or Dessert Wine

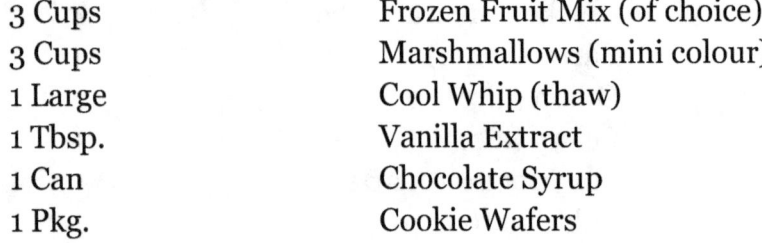

I'M BERRY MUCH IN LOVE WITH YOU

(Marshmallow & Fruit)

3 Cups	Frozen Fruit Mix (of choice)
3 Cups	Marshmallows (mini colour)
1 Large	Cool Whip (thaw)
1 Tbsp.	Vanilla Extract
1 Can	Chocolate Syrup
1 Pkg.	Cookie Wafers

1. Mix fruit, mallows and whip then refrigerate 3 hours or overnight
2. Serve mixture in dessert bowl
3. Drizzle with chocolate syrup
4. Stick cookie wafer in center of mixture
5. Serve immediately

Your first recipe is like your first date;
ample anticipation, poise confidence,
more than enough anxiety,
the equivalent amount of questionable,
and a level of excitement.

A FARE CHANCE

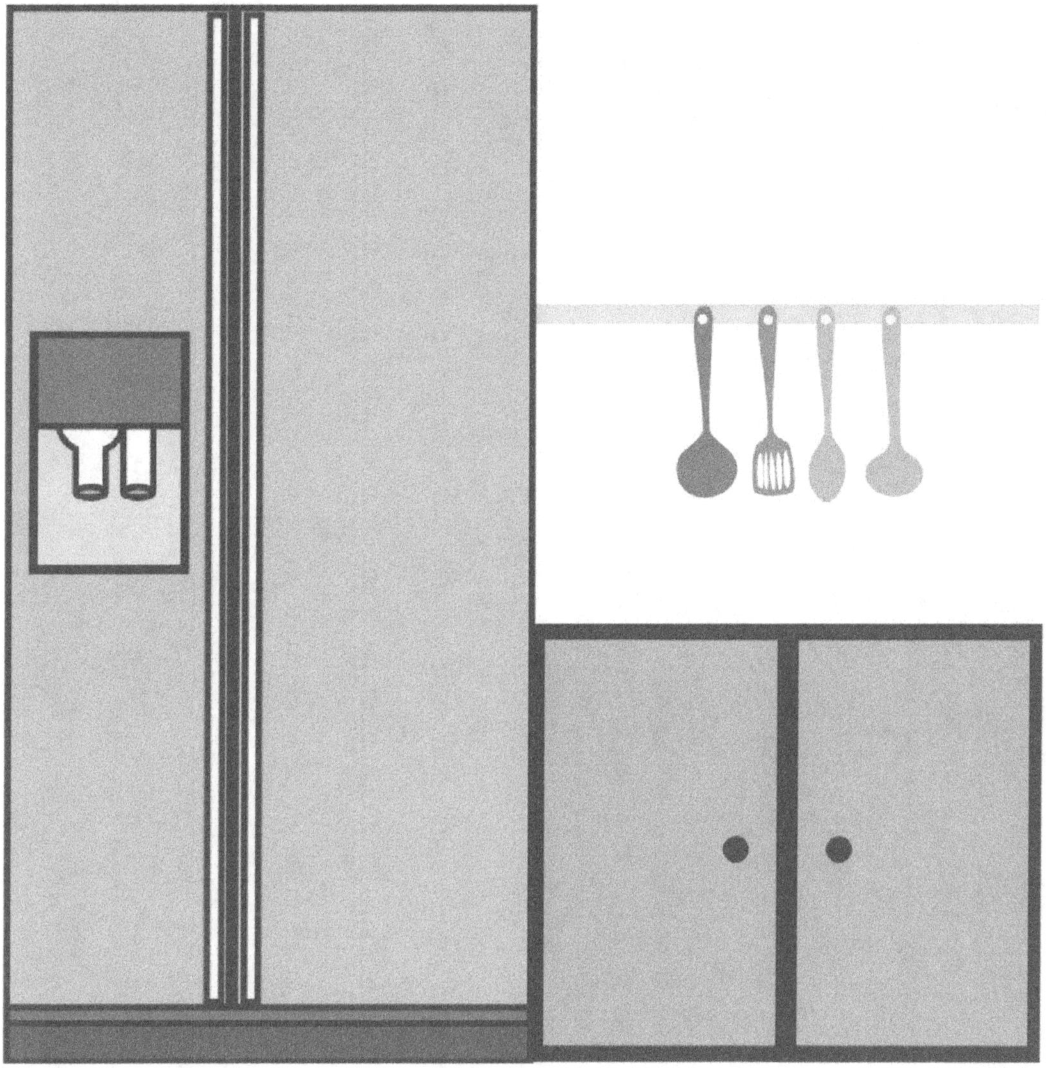

FARE HAND

A FARE CHANCE

Category: Salad
Servings: 2 to 4 guests
Prep Time: 15-20 minutes
Cooking Time: 7 minutes
Serve with: Fish or Dinner Appetizer

YOU SHRIMPLY GUAC MY WORLD

(Prawn & Avocado)

2 Cups	Prawns (cut in halves)
4 Large	Avocado's (cut into eighth's each shell half)
3 Stalks	Celery (finely dice)
½ Cup	Red Onion (finely dice)

Dressing:

2 Tbsps.	Dijon mustard
2 Tbsps.	Honey
½ Cup	Cilantro
1 Tbsp.	Habanero Chile (remove seeds & mince)
1 Cup	Mayonnaise
2 Tbsps.	Lemon Juice

Add all dressing ingredients above into a blender and blend at high speed for 2 minutes

1. Peeled and cut prawns in half
2. Cook Prawns until pink then cool
3. Cut Avocado in half and remove pit
4. Take knife and square avocado into eighths
5. Remove avocado squares from the shell
6. Add avocado, prawns, celery and red onion in a bowl
7. Add sauce to the bowl and toss gently until all is coated
8. Spoon mixture into avocado shell
9. Serve within an hour of preparation

Category: Salad
Servings: 2 to 4 guests
Prep Time: 15 minutes
Cooking Time: N/A
Serve with: Dinner

THE FLOWER OF MY LIFE
(Cauliflower & Red Pepper)

4 Cups	Cauliflower (chop)
1 Large	Red Pepper (slice)
1 Medium	White Onion (slice)

Dressing:

2 Cups	Mayonnaise
½ Cup	White Vinegar
1 Tsp.	Pepper
1 Tsp.	Seasoning Salt
1 Tsp.	Parsley

1. Prepare vegetables and toss in a salad bowl
2. Prepare and whisk dressing
3. Pour dressing then toss to coat vegetables
4. Place in fridge for at least an hour (longer is better)

Category: Salad
Servings: 3 to 4 guests
Prep Time: 10 minutes
Cooking Time: N/A
Serve with: Dinner

MR. CUKE RODE OFF ON HIS SCALLION
(Cucumber)

1 Large	English Cucumber (slice)
3 Large	Green Onions (chop both white & green parts)

Dressing:

1 Cup	Sour Cream
¼ Cup	Mayonnaise
2 Tbsps.	Malt Vinegar
1 Tsp.	Dill Weed (dry)
1 Tsp.	Seasoning Salt

1. Prepare vegetables
2. Prepare and whisk dressing
3. Pour dressing then toss to coat vegetables in bowl
4. Place in fridge until ready to serve

Category: Salad
Servings: 4 to 6 guests
Prep Time: 20 minutes
Cooking Time: 15 minutes
Serve with: Meat or Fish

YOU ARE MY SLHAM DUNK

(Ham Greek Pasta)

5 Cups	Orzo Pasta
1 Cup	Green Pepper (finely dice)
1 Cup	Red or White Onion (finely dice)
1 Cup	Tomato (finely dice)
1 Cup	English Cucumber (finely dice)
½ Cup	Black Olives (finely chop)
2 Cups	Feta Cheese (crumble)
2 Cups	Ham (cube)

Dressing:

1 Cup	Olive Oil
¼ Cup	White Vinegar
¼ Cup	White Wine
3 Tbsps.	Lemon Juice
½ Tsp.	Basil (dry)
½ Tsp.	Parsley (dry)
½ Tsp.	Garlic (dry mince)

1. Cook pasta per package instructions
2. Once cooked rinse under cold water
3. Place pasta in big bowl
4. Add all vegetables, olives and cheese to pasta
5. Prepare and whisk dressing
6. Add dressing to pasta and toss to coat
7. Refrigerate 1 hour for pasta to marinade in the dressing
8. Then toss once again before serving

Category: Salad
Servings: 3 to 4 guests
Prep Time: 25 minutes
Cooking Time: 30 minutes
Serve with: Meat or Fish

HE SPUDDER HER NAME BACONING MY HEART
(Potato)

8 Cups	Chicken Stock
4 Large	Potatoes (boil & cube)
4 Slices	Bacon (fried & chop)
2 Large	Celery sticks (slice)
1 Large	Onion (chop)
4 Large	Radishes (slice)
1 Large	Green Pepper (slice)
1 Large	Red Pepper (slice)
2 Large	Eggs (boil & chop)

Dressing:

1 Cup	Mayonnaise
3 Tbsps.	White Vinegar
½ Cup	Vegetable Oil
2 Tbsps.	Dijon Mustard
1 Tbsp.	Seasoning Salt
1 Tbsp.	Garlic (dry mince)
¼ Cup	Parsley (dry)
1 Tbsp.	Pepper

1. Wash the Potatoes clean
2. Boil potatoes in chicken stock or water until tender
3. Remove from stock or water and cool potatoes to room temperature
4. Peel and cube potatoes then place in a large bowl
5. Add all prepared vegetables in with potatoes
6. Ad bacon and eggs
7. Prepare and whisk dressing
8. Add dressing to potato salad and toss until coated
9. Refrigerate for two hours before serving

Category: Salad
Servings: 2 to 4 guests
Prep Time: 30 minutes
Cooking Time: N/A
Serve with: Fish, Chicken, Beef, Pork

MY RAMENTIC WAYS ARE SO HOT
(Asian Noodle)

4 Pkg.	Ramen Soup Noodles (3 oz.)
1 Bunch	Green Onions (chop)
2 Cups	Green Cabbage (finely slice)
1 Large	Green Pepper (slice)
1 Large	Red Pepper (slice)
1 Stick	Celery (slice)
2 Tbsps.	Slivered Almonds (roast)
2 Tbsps.	Sesame Seeds (roast)
1 Tbsp.	Red Chili Flakes

Dressing:

1 Pkg.	Noodle Package Seasoning
1 Cup	Canola Oil
½ Cup	Hot Sauce
¼ Cup	Sesame Oil
2 Tbsps.	White Vinegar
1 Tbsp.	Sugar
3 Tbsps.	Garlic (dry mince)

1. Prepare dressing and whisk then set aside
2. Roast sesame seeds and almonds on cookie sheet @ 425° until golden
3. Add seeds and almonds to large bowl
4. Break up noodles inside their package then add to bowl
5. Prepare & add all salad ingredients to bowl
6. Add dressing to noodle mix toss until all coated
7. Refrigerate for 3 hours, tossing every ½ hour

Category: Salad
Servings: 4 to 6 guests
Prep Time: 25 minutes
Cooking Time: N/A
Serve with: Dinner or Dinner Appetizer

MY TUNAVERSE HAS ALWAYS BEEN YOU
(Sashimi Mix)

1 ½ Cups	Sashimi Tuna (dice)
1 Cup	Green Onions (dice)
2 Tbsps.	Sesame Seeds (roast)
½ Cup	Lime Juice
1 Tbsp.	Ginger (grate)
2 Tbsps.	Soya Sauce
1 Tbsp.	Sesame Seed Oil
1 Cup	Avocado's (mash)
½ Tsp.	Wasabi Paste
1 Large	Butter Lettuce (wash & chop)

Dressing:

2 Tbsp.	Dijon mustard
2 Tbsp.	Honey
¼ Cup	Cilantro
1 Cup	Mayonnaise
1 Large	Lime (Juice)

1. Mix the first eight ingredients together then refrigerate for 2 hours
2. Peel & mash avocado adding Wasabi paste then blend into a creamy paste
3. Add paste to tuna mixture
4. Place greens on plate
5. Scoop tuna mixture on to middle of greens
6. Keep refrigerate until serving
7. When serving drizzle dressing on tuna and greens

Category: Salad
Servings: 3 to 4 guests
Prep Time: 15 minutes
Cooking Time: N/A
Serve with: Dinner

OUR HEARTS ROMAINE IN LOVE
(Romaine & Artichoke)

6 Cups	Romaine (chop)
2 Cups	Artichoke Hearts (chop)
1 Cup	Croutons
½ Cup	Red Onion (finely slice)
1 Cup	Parmesan Cheese (shave)

Caesar Dressing

½ Large	Lemon (juice)
1 Cup	Extra Virgin Olive Oil
2 Large	Eggs (Room Temperature)
1 Large	Garlic Clove (mashed)
1 Tbsp.	Capers
1 Tbsp.	Dijon Mustard
1 Tbsp.	Anchovy Paste
2 Tbsps.	Worcestershire Sauce
½ Cup	Parmesan Cheese
½ Tsp.	Parsley (dry)
1 Tsp.	Pepper

1. Combine all salad ingredients into Bowl
2. Add all ingredients to a blender and blend at high until creamy
3. Refrigerate dressing for an hour or overnight
4. Add dressing to greens and toss
5. Serve immediately

Category: Salad
Servings: 4 to 6 guests
Prep Time: 20 minutes
Cooking Time: N/A
Serve with: Dinner

YOU ARE THE STAR IN MY LIFE
(Fruit)

1 Large	Banana (slice thinly)
2 Large	Kiwi (chop)
½ Large	Pineapple (core & chop)
1 Large	Star Fruit (slice thinly)
1 Cup	Cherries (remove pit)
1 Large	Mango (cut into chunks)
1 Cup	Strawberries (slice)
1 Large	Avocado (chop)
1 Cup	Walnuts (crumble & roast)
1 Cup	Feta Cheese (crumble)

Dressing

1 Large	Lemon (juice)
½ Cup	Avocado Oil
¼ Cup	Honey (melt)
½ Tsp.	Mint (mince)

1. Prepare and combine salad ingredients
2. Prepare and whisk dressing
3. Add dressing to salad
4. Refrigerate for ½ hour then serve

Category: Salad
Servings: 4 to 6 guests
Prep Time: 20 minutes
Cooking Time: N/A
Served with: Entrée

WE HAVE THE SLAW OF ATTRACTION
(Cole Slaw)

4 Cups	Green Cabbage (chop finely or grate)
1 Cup	Onion (finely)

Dressing

½ Cup Sour Cream
1 Cup Mayonnaise
1 Tbsp Malt Vinegar
3 Tbsp White Sugar

1. Rinse & dry cabbage
2. Add onion
3. Prepare and whisk dressing
4. Add dressing to cabbage mix and toss
5. Refrigerate for 2 hours tossing every ½ hour
6. Serve with dinner

Category: Salad
Servings: 4 to 6 guests
Prep Time: 25 minutes
Cooking Time: 15 minutes
Serve with: Fish, Chicken or Bread

CELERYBRATING THE PASTABILITY OF FOREVER LOVE
(Veggie Pasta)

4 Cups	Uncooked Pasta (Penne)
1 Medium	Red or White Onion (dice)
4 Sticks	Asparagus (chop in half inch pieces)
1 Cup	Red Pepper (dice)
1 Cup	Green Pepper (dice)
½ Medium	Zucchini (dice)
2 Stalks	Celery (chop)
1 Cup	Broccoli (chop)
1 Cup	Cauliflower (chop)
1 Cup	Parmesan Cheese (or your choice)
1 Cup	Caesar Dressing
½ Cup	Italian Dressing

1. Cook pasta as per package instructions
2. Rinse pasta under cold water and set aside
3. Break off tough end of asparagus
4. Toss asparagus into boiling water remove when bright green into ice water
5. Remove from ice water and cut into half inch pieces
6. Prepare salad vegetables and add to pasta then toss
7. Add salad dressings and toss until coated
8. Refrigerate for 1 or more hours

FARE PLAY

A FARE CHANCE

Category: Entree
Servings: 3 to 4 guests
Prep Time: 25 minutes
Cooking Time: 25 to 35 minutes
Serve with: Bread & Salad

MS. RICE RUMORED IN A SPANISH A FARE
(Paella)

3 Cups	Minute Rice (cooked)
6 Large	Chicken Wing Drumettes
1 Large	Italian Sausage (slice)
8 Large	Prawns
6 Large	Frozen Kiwi Mussels or ½ pound of regular mussels
½ Pkg.	Seafood Mix
½ Medium	Red Pepper (finely slice)
½ Medium	Green Pepper (finely slice)
1 Medium	Onion (finely slice)
1 Cup	Frozen Peas
1 Cup	Salsa (from a jar)
2 Cups	Chicken Broth
1 Cup	White Wine
½ Cup	Olive Oil
1 Cup	Butter (cut into squares)
1 Tbsp.	Turmeric Powder

1. Cook rice to package instructions adding turmeric powder to water
2. Roast chicken wings in oven at 350 until golden
3. Fry peppers, onion and sausage in olive oil
4. Except for mussels and butter add all ingredients in a deep roasting pan
5. Toss until completely blended
6. Place mussels open side into the rice mixture or if using regular mussels just place over top of rice
7. Place butter squares on top of rice mixture equally apart
8. Cover roasting pan with foil
9. Bake in 350° preheated oven for 25 minutes
10. Serve immediately

Category: Entree
Servings: 2 to 4 guests
Prep Time: 15 minutes
Cooking Time: 20 minutes
Serve with: Pasta

WOULD BE GRATE IF WE DO DINNER TOMATO
(Beef & Tomato)

2 Pounds	Ground Beef
1 Large	Onion (dice)
2 Cups	Can Tomatoes (dice)
3 Large	Mushrooms (slice)
1 Tsp.	Garlic (mince)
1 Cup	Parmesan Cheese

1. Cook beef until brown
2. Cook onions and mushrooms until tender
3. Add all ingredients to ground beef and toss
4. Cook pasta to package instructions
5. Rinse cook pasta and toss in beef mixture
6. Sprinkle with shaved parmesan cheese when serving

Category: Entree
Servings: 6 to 8 guests
Prep Time: 25 minutes
Cooking Time: 1.5 hours
Serve with: Toss Salad & French Bread

IF YOU'RE CHILI I KNOW HOW TO HEAT YOU UP
(Chili)

2 Pounds	Ground Beef
1 Large	Green Pepper (dice)
1 Large	Onion (dice)
2 Dozen	Small Mushrooms (cut in half)
4 Stalks	Celery (chop)
7 Strips	Bacon (chop)
2-16 Ounce	Red Kidney Beans
1-16 Ounce	Tomatoes (dice)
2 Cups	Beer
1-8 Ounce	Tomato Soup
2 Tbsps.	Tomato Paste
1/3 Cup	Chili Powder
3 Tbsps.	Garlic (dry mince)
2 Tbsps.	Seasoning Salt
3 Tbsps.	Parsley (dry)

1. Cook beef until brown
2. Cook bacon then crumble into beef
3. Add all remaining ingredients and toss
4. Cover on low to medium heat for 60 minutes tossing every 15 minutes
5. Turn to low heat until ready to serve

Category: Entree
Servings: 3 to 4 guests
Prep Time: 20 minutes
Cooking Time: 35 minutes
Serve with: Salad

MR. SHEP HERD I ONLY HAVE PIES FOR YOU
(Shepherd Pie)

2 Tbsps.	Canola Oil
2 Pounds	Ground Beef
1 Large	Onion (dice)
2 Stalks	Celery (dice)
4 Large	Mushrooms (thinly slice)
5 Large	Russet Potatoes (peel and cut into cubes)
3 Tbsps.	Butter
½ Cup	Mayonnaise
½ Cup	Sour Cream
2 Cans	Crème Corn
¼ Cup	Worcestershire Sauce
2 Tbsps.	Granulated Garlic
1 Tbsp.	Seasoning Salt

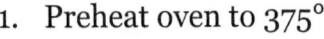

1. Preheat oven to 375°
2. Boil potatoes in water and cook until tender then drain
3. Mash the potatoes
4. Add mayo, sour crème, butter, and granulated garlic to potatoes and blend
5. Set potatoes aside
6. In a large sauté pan over medium-high heat add oil, onion, celery and mushrooms and cook until tender
7. Sauté beef until brown in colour
8. Add vegetables, salt, and sauce to beef
9. Pour the mixture into a 1 1/2-quart baking dish
10. Pour the crème corn over the meat mixture
11. Spread mashed potatoes over the corn and meat mixture
12. Smooth the potatoes then crosshatch the top with a fork
13. Bake until golden
14. Serve immediately

Category: Entree
Servings: 3 to 4 guests
Prep Time: 10 minutes
Cooking Time: 30 minutes
Serve with: Salad

MY CHICK WAS STEWING FOR HOURS
(Chicken Stew)

8	Chicken Thighs
6 Large	Carrots (peel & quarter)
5 Large	Potatoes (peel & quarter)
1 Large	Onion (quarter)
4 Slices	Bacon (chop)
2 Tbsps.	Garlic (mince)
1 Tbsp.	Seasoning Salt
4 Cups	Water

1. Cook and chop bacon then set aside
2. Prepare your vegetables
3. Heat frying pan until hot (*try the water drops test)
4. Place and sear chicken thighs skin down until they loosen from the pan
5. Cook other side of thighs for about 2 minutes
6. Place all the vegetables and bacon around chicken
7. Add water to chicken mixture
8. Season with garlic and salt
9. Cover and put on low to med for about 30 minutes
10. Serve immediately

*Throw a few drops of water into the frying pan if they bubble and disappear you're frying pan is ready to sear the meat.

Category: Entree
Servings: 6 to 8 guests
Prep Time: 30 minutes
Cooking Time: 1 hour
Serve with: Garlic Bread

MY MISTEAK WAS NOT LOVING VEGIE MORE
(Vegetable Lasagna)

9 Strips	Lasagna Noodles or 3 Large Eggplant (slice lengthwise thinly)
1 Large	Zucchini (slice)
8 Large	Mushrooms (slice)
1 Large	Green Pepper (slice)
3 Stalks	Celery (dice)
3 Medium	Carrots (thinly slice)
2 Medium	Onions (thinly slice)
2 Cups	Diced Tomatoes (drain)
2 Pkgs.	Frozen Spinach (dry)
5 Cups	Mozzarella Cheese (grate)
3 Cups	Parmesan Cheese (shave)
2 Cups	Old Cheddar Cheese (grate)
3 Cups	Pizza Sauce
4 Cups	Spaghetti Sauce
3 Tbsp.	Garlic (dry mince)
1 Cup	Basil (chop)
3 Tbsp.	Oregano Spice
2 Tbsp.	Seasoning Salt

1. Cook lasagna noodles as per packaged instructions, cool and set aside
2. Eggplant bake in 400° oven for 20 minutes take out and cool then dab dry
3. Toss the cheeses together in a separate bowl and set aside
4. Thaw spinach and squeeze excess water out of spinach
5. Cook all vegetables lightly and cool
6. Add the spinach and drained tomatoes to cooked vegetables and toss
7. Add the sauces, garlic, basil, oregano, and salt to vegetables and toss
8. Spread vegetable mixture on bottom on lasagna pan
9. Layer with noodles (three strips)
10. Spread vegetable mixture over noodles
11. Layer cheeses over the vegetable mixture about 2 ½ cups
12. Continue pattern for two more layers
13. Top with the remaining cheese mixture and cover with foil
14. Bake in preheated oven 375° for 45 minutes and uncovered for 15 minutes

Category: Entree
Servings: 2 to 4 guests
Prep Time: 10 minutes
Cooking Time: 20 to 25 minutes
Serve with: Polish Sausage & Toss Salad

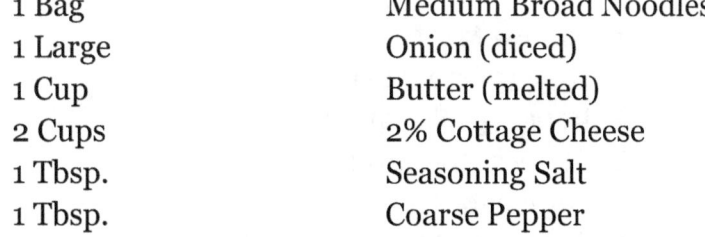

PASTABLY A WEEKEND AT MY COTTAGE
(Koluski)

1 Bag	Medium Broad Noodles
1 Large	Onion (diced)
1 Cup	Butter (melted)
2 Cups	2% Cottage Cheese
1 Tbsp.	Seasoning Salt
1 Tbsp.	Coarse Pepper

1. Melt butter
2. Cook onion in butter until tender
3. Cook noodles per instructions on package
4. Rinse and drain noodles once cooked and toss into a roasting pan
5. Add cheese, onions, salt, pepper, and toss together
6. Cover with foil place in preheated oven 350° for 20 minutes
7. Serve immediately

Category: Entree
Servings: 4 to 6 guests
Prep Time: 30 minutes
Cooking Time: 2 hours
Serve with: Salad & French Bread

ROOTING FOR ME IS BETTER THAN WINEING
(Beef Stew)

4 pounds	Beef Stew Meat
6 Large	Carrots (peel & quarter)
6 Large	Potatoes (peel & quarter)
1 Can	Tomatoes (16 oz. diced)
2 Cups	Turnip (cubes)
3 Large	Onions (quartered)
8 Large	Mushrooms (halved)
2 Cups	Frozen Peas
2 Cups	Cabbage (sliced)
2 Tbsps.	Butter (melted)
2 Cups	Red Wine
4 Cups	Water
½ Cup	Fresh Parsley (chopped)
2 Tbsps.	Dry Thyme
2 Large	Bay Leaf's

1. Melt butter in a large pot
2. Add meat and sear on all sides
3. Add veggies except for cabbage and frozen peas
4. Then add tomatoes, wine, water, and herbs
5. Bring to a boil on high heat
6. Covered pot then lower heat to medium low for one hour
7. Add frozen peas and cabbage and cover for 1 hour on low heat

Category: Entree
Servings: 2 to 4 guests
Prep Time: 20 minutes
Cooking Time: 45 minutes
Serve with: A Salad

BELLA WANT TO MEAT MR. RICE GUY
(Stuffed Peppers)

1 Pound	Ground Meat (beef, chicken or lamb)
1 Medium	Onion (diced)
2 Large	Mushrooms (sliced)
1 Stalk	Celery (diced)
1 Large	Tomato (finely diced)
2 Large	Green Peppers
1 Cup	Rice (long grain)
1 Can	Cheese or Celery Soup
½ Cup	White Wine
2 Tbsps.	Garlic (dry minced)
½ Tsp.	Chili Pepper Flakes
3 Tbsps.	Olive Oil
1 Tsp.	Seasoning Salt
1 Cup	Parmesan Cheese

1. Cook rice as per package instructions
2. Cook vegetables in oil until tender and set aside
3. Brown meat and set aside
4. Combine rice, vegetables, meat, wine, seasonings, salt and toss
5. Cut top off green peppers, clean inside, rinse and pat dry
6. Fill green peppers with meat and rice mixture to the top
7. Arrange on roasting pan
8. Cover with tin foil
9. Bake in preheated 350° oven
10. Bake for 45 minutes or until peppers are tender
11. Heat soup to bubbling point stirring continuously
12. Place green pepper on plate
13. Pour ¼ cup of soup over each pepper
14. Top ½ cup of cheese on each pepper
15. Serve immediately

For Vegetarians it tastes great without meat as well.

Category: Entree
Servings: 3 to 4 guests
Prep Time: 15 minutes
Cooking Time: 25 to 35 minutes
Serve with: Rice & Salad

PRAWNISE I WON'T BACON YOUR HEART

(Curry Prawns)

16 Large	Prawns (halved)
1 Large	Onion (chopped)
1 Large	Red Pepper (sliced thinly)
1 Large	Green Pepper (sliced thinly)
2 Stalks	Celery (chopped)
5 Strips	Bacon (chopped)
1 Tbsp.	Ginger (finely chopped)
1 Tbsp.	Garlic (minced)
1 Cup	White Wine
2 Cups	Chicken Broth
2 Cups	Crème
1 Cup	Butter (melted)
¼ Cup	Curry Powder
2 Tbsps.	White Sugar
3 Tbsps.	Flour
3 Cups	Rice (uncooked)

1. Cook rice to package instructions
2. Fry Bacon and chop then set aside
3. In same pan add butter to cook vegetables, ginger and garlic until tender
4. Add bacon, curry powder, sugar, and flour then stir to form a paste
5. Add chicken broth and wine to vegetable paste whisking vigorously until liquid thickens
6. Add crème, whisk until thickens then turn down to low heat
7. If curry sauce gets too thick just add more crème
8. Add shrimp and toss until pink then serve over rice

Category: Entree
Servings: 2 to 4 guests
Prep Time: 3 to 4 hours
Cooking Time: 45
Serve with: Roasted Potatoes & Vegetables

YOU RIB ME ABOUT YOUR SAUCY WAY
(Beef Ribs)

3 Pounds	Beef or Pork Spareribs

Marinade

2 Cups	Soya Sauce
2 Cups	Red Wine
2 Cups	White Sugar or 3 Cups of Brown Sugar
2 Tsps.	Chili Flakes
3 Tbsps.	Garlic (dry minced)
3 Tbsps.	Onion (dry minced)
2 Tbsps.	Parsley (dry)
1 Cup	Water

1. Whisk marinade ingredients
2. Pour marinade in a Ziploc bag along with short ribs
3. Make sure meat is soaking in marinade
4. Refrigerate for 3 hours
5. Remove ribs from marinade and place in roasting pan
6. Set aside remaining marinade
7. Add water to bottom of pan
8. Cover with foil and bake preheated 350° for 1 hour
9. Uncover and pour remaining marinade over ribs
10. Bake for an additional 20 minutes uncover
11. Serve immediately

Category: Entree
Servings: 2 to 4 guests
Prep Time: 25 minutes
Cooking Time: 45 minutes
Serve with: Salad

IT'S OFFISHIAL I WANT TO MAYO YOU

(Salmon Loaf)

4 Cups	Baked Salmon (flaked)
1 Large	Baked Potato (sliced thinly)
1 Large	Tomato (sliced thinly)
1 Cup	Breadcrumbs
½ Cup	Flour
¼ Cup	Onion (diced)
¼ Cup	Jalapeno (diced)
½ Cup	Green Pepper (diced)
½ Cup	Red Pepper (diced)
½ Cup	Celery (diced)
2 Large	Eggs (beaten)
2 Tbsps.	Worcestershire sauce
1 Tbsp.	Cilantro (dry)
1 Tsp.	Dill Weed (dry)
1 Tbsp.	Garlic (minced)
2 Tsps.	Dijon Mustard
3 Tbsps.	Mayonnaise
1 Tsp.	Seasoning Salt
1 Tsp.	Pepper

1. Preheat oven 350°
2. Set aside sliced potato and tomato
3. Flake baked salmon in a bowl
4. Add the rest of the ingredients to the salmon
5. Toss the salmon and ingredients
6. Add the 1/3 of the salmon mixture to the bottom of the loaf pan
7. Layer sliced potato over salmon mixture
8. Spread another 1/3 of salmon mixture over potatoes
9. Layer sliced tomato over salmon mixture
10. Top with remaining salmon mixture
11. Baked uncovered for 20 minutes
12. Let the loaf rest for 5 minutes before serving

Category: Entree
Servings: 3 to 6 guests
Prep Time: 20 minutes
Cooking Time: 15 to 20 minutes
Serve with: Salad

OUR LOVE HAS MUSHROOM OVER THE YEARS
(Baked Stuffed Mushrooms)

6 Large	Portobello Mushrooms
2 Cups	Plain Philadelphia Crème Cheese
1 Cup	Philadelphia Crème Cheese (smoked salmon)
½ Cup	Onion (diced)
1 Cup	Breadcrumbs
2 Tbsps.	Garlic (minced)
2 Tbsps.	Worcestershire sauce
8 Large	Prawns (chopped)
½ Cup	Butter
1 Cup	Mozzarella Cheese (grated)
1 cup	Parmesan cheese (shaved)

1. Wash the mushrooms & remove stems
2. Dice finely mushrooms stems
3. Add diced onion to mushrooms and toss
4. Melt 2 tbsp. of butter add mushroom mix and garlic cook until tender
5. Chopped Prawns
6. Spray baking dish with butter
7. Mix all ingredients together except parmesan cheese
8. Top portobello mushroom prawn and cheese mixture
9. Greased baking dish with butter
10. Place mushroom caps on baking dish
11. Sprinkle the parmesan cheese on stuffed mushroom caps
12. Bake preheated 350° oven for 15 to 20 minutes or until cheese is golden then serve immediately

Category: Entree
Servings: 1 to 2 guests
Prep Time: 3 ½ hours
Cooking Time: 2 to 3 hours
Serve with: Rice & Vegetable

I'M SOYA NUTS OVER YOU
(Thai Ribs)

1 rack	Pork Ribs

Marinade

3 Tbsps.	Garlic (minced)
3 Tbsps.	Ginger (grated)
2 Tbsps.	Peanut Butter (melted)
½ Cup	Lime Juice
2 Cups	Coconut Milk
1 Cup	Soya Sauce
1 Tbsp.	Sesame Seeds (roasted)
1 Cup	White Sugar
1 Cup	Cilantro (chopped finely)

1. Add marinade ingredients to a pot
2. Bring marinade to a boil while whisking
3. Set marinade aside and let cool
4. Pour cool marinade into a Ziploc bag then ribs
5. Marinade and refrigerate for 3 hours
6. Place ribs and sauce in a roasting pan and cover with foil
7. Bake in 350° oven for 2 hours
8. Remove foil and bake for another ½ hour
9. Serve immediately

Category: Entree
Servings: 1 to 2 guests
Prep Time: 15 minutes
Cooking Time: 15 to 20 minutes
Serve with: Roasted Potatoes & Vegetable

YOU'RE SALMON TO ADOUGH

(Phyllo wrapped Salmon)

2	Salmon Fillets (6 oz. each)
6 Sheets	Phyllo Pastry
1 Tbsp	Lemon Juice
1 Cup	Butter (melted)
1 Tbsp.	Dill Weed (dry)
1 Tbsp.	Garlic (dry minced)
1 Tbsp.	Onion (dry minced)
1 Tsp.	Seasoning Salt

1. Three sheets to every salmon fillet
2. Melt Butter and cool
3. Brush each sheet with butter and place on a buttered sheet & repeat
4. Place fillet in center of pastry
5. Sprinkle with lemon juice then dill, onion, garlic and seasoning salt
6. Wrap fillet and fold under
7. Place folded side of pastry on a greased cookie sheet
8. Place in a preheated oven 400° for 10 to 15 minutes or until pastry is golden and flaky

Category: Entree
Servings: 6 to 8 guests
Prep Time: 20 to 25 minutes
Cooking Time: 1 to 1.15 hours
Serve with: Salad & Garlic Bread

PASTABILIY YOU'LL BAKE MY HEART
(Baked Lasagna)

9 Strips	Lasagna Noodles
2 Cups	Frozen Spinach (thawed)
3 Pounds	Beef or Chicken (minced)
1 Medium	Green Pepper (diced)
1 Medium	Onion (diced)
6 Large	Mushrooms (diced)
3 Tbsps.	Garlic (minced)
1 Can	Crushed Tomatoes (9 oz.)
1 Can	Pizza Sauce (9 oz.)
1 Cup	2% Cottage Cheese
6 Cups	Mozzarella (grated)
2 Cups	Parmesan Cheese (shredded)
½ Cup	Olive Oil
2 Tbsps.	Oregano (dry)
2 Tbsps.	Basil (dry)
2 Tbsps.	Chili Flakes (dry)
2 Tbsps.	Parsley (dry)
2 Tbsps.	Seasoning Salt

1. Cook lasagna noodles as per packaged instructions
2. Rinse noodles under cold water until cool and set aside
3. Rinse spinach under hot water until thawed & squeeze excess water
4. Fry meat & vegetables in oil until tender
5. In a bowl mix all ingredients except for Mozzarella & Parmesan
6. In a separate bowl mix cheese's
7. Spread meat sauce on bottom of lasagna pan
8. Layer three strips of noodles over meat sauce
9. Spread meat sauce over noodles then cover with cheese mixture
10. Continue pattern times 2
11. Topped with cheese mixture
12. Cover with foil and bake 350° preheated for 45 to 60 minutes
13. Uncover and bake for an additional 15 minutes (make sure pan is on second oven rack)
14. Ready to serve

Category: Entree
Servings: 2 to 4 guests
Prep Time: 7 to 10 minutes
Cooking Time: 10 to 15 minutes
Served with: Cheesy Mash Potatoes & Vegetable

YOU'RE SALMON WHOSE BUTTER THAN ME
(Baked Salmon)

1 Large	Salmon Rack (half-side)
½ Cup	Butter (melted)
½ Cup	White Wine
¼ Cup	Lemon Juice
1 Tbsp.	Garlic (minced)
1 Tbsp.	Onion (minced)
1 Tbsp.	Seasoning Salt
1 Tbsp.	Dill Weed (dry)

1. Place salmon in a greased baking pan
2. Pour wine over salmon
3. Melt butter pour over salmon
4. Sprinkle lemon juice over salmon
5. Sprinkle garlic, seasoning salt, onion then dill in that order
6. Place in oven at 350° for 10 to 15 minutes or until flaky
7. Serve immediately

Category: Entree
Servings: 3 to 4 guests
Prep Time: 25 minutes
Cooking Time: 35 to 50 minutes
Serve with: Cornbread & Salad

YOUR SPICY SCENT IS SEDUCING

(Cajun Jambalaya)

3 Cups	Minute Rice (uncooked)
1 Large	Chicken Breast (chopped)
1 Ring	Ukrainian Sausage (sliced)
12 Large	Prawns (halved)
1 Medium	Red Pepper (chopped)
1 Medium	Green Pepper (chopped)
2 Stalks	Celery (chopped)
1 Medium	Onion (chopped)
1 Cup	Can Diced Tomatoes
1 Large	Jalapeno (finely chopped)
¼ Cup	Olive Oil
4 Cups	Chicken Broth
1 Cup	Butter (melted)
3 Tbsps.	Parsley (dry)
1 Tbsps.	Cayenne Pepper
1 Tbsp.	Cajun Spice
2 Tbsps.	Garlic (minced)
1 Cup	Green Onions (chopped)

1. Follow package directions for rice (use chicken broth instead of water)
2. Fry chicken, peppers, celery, onion, and sausage in olive oil
3. Add all the ingredients into a casserole dish except green onions
4. Add 1 Cup of chicken broth and mix until completely blended
5. Cover with foil
6. Bake 350° preheated oven for 20 to 35 minutes or until liquid is absorb
7. Sprinkle with green onions
8. Serve immediately

Category: Entree
Servings: 6-8 people
Prep Time: 20 minutes
Cooking Time: 20 to 25 minutes
Serve with: Salad & Condiments

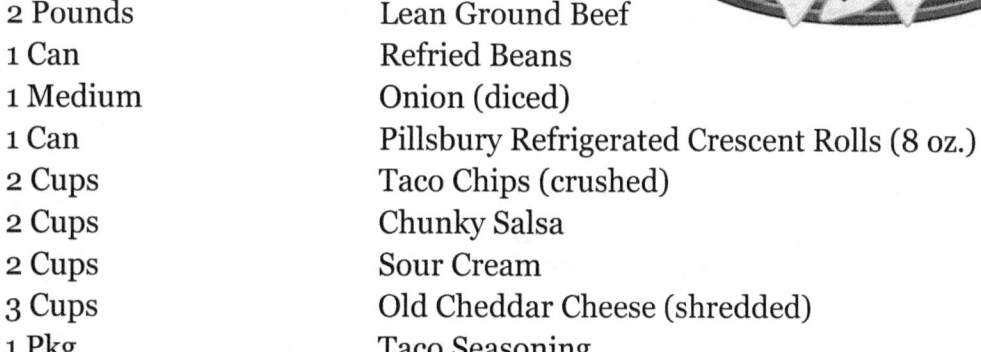

TACO 'BOUT LOVING YOU
(Taco Pie)

2 Pounds	Lean Ground Beef
1 Can	Refried Beans
1 Medium	Onion (diced)
1 Can	Pillsbury Refrigerated Crescent Rolls (8 oz.)
2 Cups	Taco Chips (crushed)
2 Cups	Chunky Salsa
2 Cups	Sour Cream
3 Cups	Old Cheddar Cheese (shredded)
1 Pkg.	Taco Seasoning

Condiments

4 Cups	Avocado Salsa
2 Cups	Green Onions (chopped)
2 Cups	Black Olives (thinly sliced)

1. Preheat oven to 375°F
2. Add two tbsps. of oil, ground beef, onion and taco seasoning into a large skillet and cook until done
3. Drain excess oil off meat mixture then set aside
4. Separate crescent dough into 8 triangles and place triangles in ungreased 9 or 10-inch pie pan pressing to form crust
5. Sprinkle chips over bottom of crust and press into the dough
6. Pour refried beans evenly spread over chips and dough
7. Add ground meat mixture evenly spread
8. Add chunky salsa evenly spread
9. Pour sour cream over meat mixture and evenly spread
10. Sprinkle cheese evenly on top of sour cream
11. Bake for 20 to 25 minutes or until crust is golden brown
12. Cut into wedges and serve

Category: Entree
Servings: 2 to 4 guests
Prep Time: 5 to 10 minutes
Cooking Time: 15 to 20 minutes
Serve with: Potato & Salad

I STEAK MY HEART ON YOUR LOVE
(Steak Au Poivre)

4-8 Ounces	Tenderloin Steaks (1 ½ inches thick)
4 Tbsps.	Coarse Black Pepper
4 Tsps.	Coarse Salt
4 Tbsps.	Unsalted Butter
2 Cups	Heavy Cream
⅔ Cup	Brandy or Cognac
2 Tbsps.	Dijon Mustard

1. Season steak with salt and pepper coating entire steak, press seasoning into the meat
2. Heat pan on medium high heat (sprinkle water into pan and if it bubbles away, the pan is ready)
3. Place the steak into pan and sear for 4 minutes on each side for medium-rare
4. Once desired doneness transfer to cutting board
5. Reduce heat to medium
6. Add brandy and scrape bottom of pan
7. Add cream. Dijon, butter and whisk until all combines
8. Cook until it thickens about 4 to 6 minutes
9. Sauce should coat back of a spoon
10. Plate steak sliced or not and spoon sauce over steak and serve
11. Once rested, slice steak into ½-inch pieces. Pour cream sauce over the top and serve.

Category: Entree
Servings: 4 to 6 guests
Prep Time: 15 minutes
Cooking Time: 25 to 30 minutes
Serve with: Couscous, Salad & Bread

YOU LEAVE ME SPEACHLESS
(Moroccan Chicken)

8	Chicken Thighs
½ Cup	Olive Oil
1 Cup	Peach Jam
1 Cup	Chicken Broth
½ Cup	Honey
¼ Cup	Lemon Juice
2 Cups	Tomato (diced)
1 Cup	Chickpeas (can & drained)
1 Cup	Green Olives
3 Cups	Carrots (sliced)
1 Tbsp.	Hungarian Paprika
1 Tbsp.	Garlic (granulated)
1 Tbsp.	Onion (minced)
½ Tsp.	Cinnamon
1 Tsp.	Cloves, Mint (dry), Ginger (grated), Cayenne & Cumin
1 Tbsp.	Fresh Parsley & Cilantro (chopped)

1. Add broth, jam, honey, lemon, and tomato into pot
2. Whisking on medium heat until liquified
3. Combine all herbs and spices excluding parsley and cilantro in a bowl
4. Coat Chicken in spice mix and place on a plate
5. Pour Oil in Dutch oven
6. Heat oil on medium heat for about 1 minute
7. Place chicken skin down in oil and brown then flip an do the other side
8. Pour broth and jam mixture over chicken
9. Add carrots, olives, and chickpeas
10. Sprinkle the rest of the spices over the chicken mixture
11. Cover Dutch oven for 25 to 30 minutes or until chicken is done
12. Serve chicken mixture on platter then drizzle left over sauce on chicken
13. Sprinkle the parsley and cilantro
14. Serve immediately with a side dish of yogurt

FAMILY AFFARE

A FARE CHANCE

FAMILY AFFARE

Family meals have always been about love in the preparation and sharing of time after a day of arranged activities. Having a family meal permits us to share the concerns of our day and taking the time to acknowledge the importance of each member of the family.

Having get-togethers with family and friends gives a sense of community and bonding through laughter and conversation while sharing in an array of fare.

Our family lives are full of happy and loving memories of food and fun.

The anticipation of the next celebration always fills my heart with warm thoughts."

EASTER SUNDAY, APRIL 8, 2007

One of our last dinner's we shared together before Chance's passing on July 28, 2007; 3 months and 3 weeks later.

A FARE CHANCE

THIS IS US

Donald & Colleen

CANADIANA DINNER

**MEATLOAF
OVEN BAKED POTATO
ROASTED VEGETABLES**

Category: Entree
Servings: 4 to 6 Servings
Prep Time: 10 minutes
Cooking Time: 45 minutes

MEATLOAF

3 Pounds	Lean ground beef
1 Cup	Breadcrumbs
½ Cup	Flour
½ cup	Onion (diced)
½ Cup	Celery (chopped)
½ Cup	Green Pepper (diced)
½ cup	Tomato (diced)
1 Large	Egg (beaten)
1 Tbsp.	Worcestershire sauce
1 Tsp.	Parsley Leaves (dry)
1 Tsp.	Oregano (dry)
1 Tsp.	Basil (dry)
1 Tsp.	Granulated Garlic
1 Tsp.	Seasoning Salt
1 Tsp.	Black Pepper

1. Preheat oven 350°
2. In a large bowl add all the above ingredients
3. Use your hands to mix ingredients together
4. Add the meat mixture to a loaf pan (4X8 Pan)
5. Pat the meat down to form evenly in pan
6. Bake uncovered for 45 minutes.
7. Let the meatloaf rest for 5-10 minutes before serving (or it may fall apart)

Gravy Tip: Cream of Celery Soup or package Béarnaise Sauce

VEGETARIAN replace beef with bake salmon flaked and replace Oregano and Basil with Cilantro and Dill Weed and add 3 tbsps. Mayonnaise and 2 eggs instead of one.

Prep Time: 5 minutes
Cooking Time: 45 minutes

OVEN BAKED POTATO

4 Large	Russet Potatoes or White Potatoes
1 Large	White Onion (4 slices)
1 Stick	Butter (cubed)
To Taste	Seasoning Salt

1. Wash and cut potatoes in half lengthwise
2. Place onion slice, butter cube in between both halves of potato
3. Season wrapped together in foil seam facing up
4. Place potato on cookie sheet
5. Bake potatoes 375° preheated oven for 45 minutes or until tender

Prep Time: 15 minutes
Cooking Time: 45 min

ROASTED VEGETABLES

2 Cups	Celery Root (peeled & cubed)
2 Cups	Hubbard Squash (peeled & cubed)
2 Cups	Green & Red Pepper (quartered)
2 Cups	Beets (cooked & quartered)
10 Large	Mushrooms (halved)
2 Large	Onion (quartered)
10 Large	Cloves of Garlic
½ Cup	Olive Oil & Balsamic Dressing
¼ Cup	Cilantro (chopped finely)
¼ Cup	Basil (chopped finely)
½ Cup	Parmesan Cheese (grated)

1. Preheated 375° oven
2. Place all the above vegetables on cookie sheet
3. Add oil, vinegar, garlic, salt and toss until coated
4. Roast for 45 minutes tossing vegetables once around 20 minutes

PARISIAN DINNER

LEMON CHICKEN
SCALLOP POTATOES
STUFFED TOMATOES

Category: Entree
Servings: 4 to 6 Servings
Prep Time: 10 minutes
Cooking Time: 30 minutes

LEMON CHICKEN BREAST

4 Large	Chicken Breasts

Marinade

1 Medium	Onion (finely diced)
½ Cup	Garlic (dry minced)
1 Tbsp.	Parsley (dry)
1 Tbsp.	Basil (dry)
1 Tbsp.	Cilantro (dry)
½ Cup	Olive Oil
¼ Cup	Lemon Juice

1. Whisk marinade ingredients in a bowl
2. Pour marinade to Ziploc bag
3. Add chicken to bag and toss
4. Refrigerate for 1 hour
5. Bake in 350° oven for 30 minutes or until cooked

Prep Time: 20 minutes
Cooking Time: 85 minutes

SCALLOP POTATOES (would go well with baked ham)

4 Large	Russet Potatoes (peeled & sliced)
1 Large	Onion (sliced)
1 Cup	Mozzarella Cheese (sliced)
1 Cup	Swiss Cheese (sliced)
1 Cup	Parmesan Cheese (grated)
2 Cups	Crème
1 Cup	Butter (melted)
1 Tbsp.	Seasoning Salt

1. Layer potato slices on bottom of roasting pan
2. Season with salt each layer
3. Layer onions over potatoes then sprinkle ½ cheese mixture
4. Another layer of potatoes and onions topped with rest of the cheese mix
5. Pour crème and butter over potatoes then cover with foil
6. Place roasting pan on cookie sheet for leakage
7. Bake 375° for 75 minutes or until potatoes are tender then discard foil
8. Place potatoes back in oven for 10 minutes or until cheese is golden

Check ½ hour into cooking to see if you need to add more milk

Prep Time: 20 minutes
Cooking Time: 30 minutes

STUFFED TOMATOES

4 Large	Tomatoes
1 Cup	Bread Crumbles
2 Large	Mushrooms (diced)
1 Large	Celery Stalk (diced)
1 Large	Onion (diced)
1 Large	Garlic Clove (minced)
½ Cup	Basil (finely chopped)
¼ Cup	Oregano (dry)
1 Cup	Parmesan Cheese (grated)
¼ Cup	Olive Oil
	Salt & Pepper to taste

1. Preheated 375° oven
2. Cut tops off tomatoes, scoop out pulp and seeds, rinse, pat dry
3. Add oil to frying pan on medium heat
4. Add vegetables and cook until tender
5. Toss vegetables into bowl of breadcrumbs, herbs, half of the cheese
6. Stuff Tomatoes with bread crumb mixture
7. Place on a cookie sheet and put in oven
8. Bake for 30 minutes
9. Top with Parmesan Cheese and bake for additional 5 minutes
10. Serve immediately

ITALIAN DINNER

CHICKEN CACCIATORE
TOSSED GREEN SALAD
GARLIC BREAD

Category: Entree
Servings: 4 to 6 Servings
Prep Time: 10 minutes
Cooking Time: 45 minutes

CHICKEN CACCIATORE

8 Pieces	Chicken Thighs
6 Large	Mushrooms (thinly sliced)
1 Large	Onion (finely diced)
3 Cups	Mozzarella Cheese (grated)
1 Cup	Parmesan Cheese (shaved)
1 Large	Italian Pasta Sauce
1 Cup	Frozen Spinach (rinsed & squeezed)
1 Tbsp.	Garlic (minced)

1. Place chicken in roasting pan
2. In a bowl add sauce, garlic, spinach, mushrooms and onion then mix
3. Pour sauce over chicken then cover with foil
4. Bake 350° for 45 minutes
5. Remove foil and sprinkle cheeses to cover chicken
6. Bake for another 10 minutes for cheese to melt
7. Prepare your pasta as to instructions on package
8. Serve pasta topped with sauce and chicken

Prep Time: 10-15 minutes
Cooking Time: N/A

TOSSED GREEN SALAD

3 cups	Mixed Greens
1 Cup	Green Onion (diced)
½ Cup	Radishes (sliced)
1 Cup	Cherry Tomatoes (halved)
1 Cup	Cucumber (diced)

Dressing

2 Tbsp.	Red Wine
2 Tbsp.	White Vinegar
½ Cup	Olive Oil
½ Tsp.	Tarragon (dry)
½ Tsp.	Parsley (dry)
½ Tsp.	Garlic (dry minced)
1 Tsp.	Onion (dry minced)

1. Whisk dressing ingredients and refrigerate
2. Prepare salad ingredients and refrigerate until serving
3. Pour dressing on greens toss and serve

Prep Time: 10 minutes
Cooking Time: 15 minutes

PIZZA BREAD

1 Large	French Loaf (Cut lengthwise)
1 Cup	Pizza Sauce
2 Tbsp.	Garlic (dry minced)
2 Tbsp.	Onion (dry minced)
1 Tbsp.	Oregano (dry)
1 Tbsp.	Basil (dry)
1 Stick	Butter (soften)
1 Cup	Parmesan Cheese (grated)
3 Cups	Mozzarella Cheese (grated)

1. Slice a French bread loaf in half lengthwise
2. Blend butter, garlic, onion, herbs, and grated parmesan cheese in a small bowl
3. Spread the garlic butter mixture on each half of bread
4. Spread the pizza sauce over the butter mixture
5. Wrap in foil
6. Bake preheated 350° 15 minutes
7. Uncover bread and sprinkle grated mozzarella cheese
8. Bake until cheese is melted
9. Cut bread halves into 8 pieces each

GRECIAN DINNER

CHICKEN TARRAGON
RICE PILAF
ZUCCHINI MIX

Category: Entree
Servings: 4 to 6 Servings
Prep Time: 10 minutes
Baking Time: 35 minutes

CHICKEN TARRAGON

4 Pieces	Chicken Breasts
1 Large	Onion (finely sliced)
1 Cup	White Wine
½ Cup	Chicken Broth
1 Cup	Cream
2 Tbsps.	Butter
1 Tsp.	Tarragon
1 Tsp.	Garlic (minced)
1 Tsp.	Seasoning Salt & Pepper

1. Cook chicken on hot skillet and brown on both sides
2. Remove chicken from skillet add onions and butter sauté until tender
3. Place chicken skin side down onto sauté onions
4. Mix rest of ingredients and pour over chicken
5. Cover and simmer for 25 minutes

Prep Time: 10 minutes
Cooking Time: 15 minutes

RICE PILAF

2 Cups	Minute Rice
2 Cups	Chicken Broth
½ Cup	Red Pepper (finely chopped)
½ Cup	Onion (finely chopped)
½ Cup	Brown Raisins (soaked)
½ Cup	Prawns (diced)

1 Cup	Chicken Broth
¼ Cup	Canola or Vegetable Oil
¼ Cup	Fresh Parsley (chopped)

1. Follow package instructions for rice and substitute broth instead of water
2. Remove raisins from water and set aside
3. Add oil to frying pan and sauté vegetable mix until tender add to cook rice
4. Add parsley, raisins and mix rice thoroughly
5. Ready to serve

Prep Time: 15 to 20 minutes
Cooking Time: 50 minutes

BREAD & RICE STUFFING

1 Pound	Pork Seasoned Sausage (cooked)
1 Cup	Onion (diced)
1 Cup	Celery (diced)
1 Cup	Mushrooms (sliced)
1 Cup	Sage (fresh & chopped)
3 Cups	Rice (cooked)
1 Loaf	Bread of Choice (moisten)
2 Tbsps.	Seasoning Salt
2 Tbsps.	Pepper

1. Cook Sausage, onion, mushrooms, and celery in a non-stick pan until cooked and add to a roasting pan
2. Add cooked rice, sage, salt, pepper and toss
3. Take handful of bread and run under water to dampen and squeeze excess water from bread and toss into roasting pan
4. Squeeze bread into rice mixture until completely blended
5. Cover roasting pan with tin foil
6. Place in preheated 350° oven for 25 to 35 minutes
7. Uncover and back for 10 to 15 minutes and serve

Prep Time: 5 minutes
Cooking Time: 10 minutes

STIR FRY ZUCCHINI MIX

1 large	Zucchini (quartered & sliced)
1 Medium	Red Onion (sliced)
6 Large	White Mushrooms
2 Tbsps.	Olive Oil
1 Tsp.	Seasoning Salt & Pepper

1. Sauté zucchini, mushrooms and onion in heated oil
2. Season & stir fry until golden and tender

AMERICANA DINNER

JACK DANIELS BAKED SALMON
CHEESE MASHED POTATOES
ASPARAGUS PARMESAN

Category: Entree
Servings: 4 to 6 Servings
Prep Time: 10 minutes
Cooking Time: 15 minutes

JACK DANIELS SALMON

1 Large	Salmon (Sockeye or Spring)

Marinade

1 Cup	Ketchup
1 Cup	Jack Daniels Whiskey
1 ½ Cups	Soya Sauce
1 Cup	Red Wine
2 Cups	White Sugar
1 Cup	Brown Sugar
2 Tbsps.	Liquid Smoke
2 Tbsps.	Hot Chili Flakes
2 Tbsps.	Garlic (minced)
2 Tbsps.	Onion (minced)

1. Whisk marinade ingredients and pour in Ziploc bag
2. Cut salmon into 1-inch steaks discarding head and fin
3. Toss salmon in bag, coat and refrigerate for 2 hours
4. Take salmon out of Bag and line in a baking dish
5. Bake in preheated 350° oven for 15 minutes or until flaky
6. Boil marinade down to half the liquid
7. Remove salmon from oven and brush marinade on salmon
8. Serve immediately

Prep Time: 10 minutes
Cooking Time: 20 minutes

CHEESE MASHED POTATOES

4 Large	Russet Potatoes
½ Cup	Cream Cheese
2 Tbsp.	Mayonnaise
¼ Cup	Sour Cream
2 Tbsp.	Butter
1 Cup	Parmesan Cheese
1 Tbsp.	Garlic (dry minced)
1 Tbsp.	Onion (dry minced)
1 Tbsp.	Parsley (dry)
¼ Cup	Basil (dry)

1. Wash potatoes, peel and cut into sixth's
2. Boiled potatoes until tender
3. Drain and mashed potatoes
4. Add remaining ingredients and mix thoroughly

Prep Time: 5 minutes
Cooking Time: 20 minutes

LEMON BUTTER BRUSSELS SPROUTS

3 Cups	Brussels Sprouts (frozen)
1 Cup	Onion (diced)
1 Cup	Mushroom (diced)
1 Cup	Lemon Juice
1 Cup	Butter (melted)
1 Tsp.	Seasoning Salt

1. Boil frozen Brussels sprouts until tender
2. Drain water and set aside Brussels sprouts
3. Pour butter in frying pan
4. Add onions and mushrooms and fry until tender
5. Add sprouts, lemon juice and salt then toss
6. Ready to serve

ASIAN DINNER

ASIAN PORK RIBS
PORK FRIED RICE
CHICKEN CHOP MEIN

Category: Entree
Servings: 4 to 6 Servings
Prep Time: 10 minutes
Cooking Time: 1 1/2 hours

ASIAN PORK RIBS

3 Slabs	Pork Ribs

Marinade

2 Cups	Soya Sauce
1 Cup	Chinese Beer
1 Cup	Dark Brown Sugar
3 Tbsp.	Garlic (minced)
2 Cups	Green Onion (chopped)
2 Tbsp.	Sesame Oil
2 Tbsp.	Chili Flakes

1. Whisk marinade ingredients and pour in roasting pan
2. Place ribs meat side down in roasting pan
3. Cover tightly with foil and bake 350° oven for 45 minutes
4. Turn with bone side down, cover and bake for another 45 minutes

Prep Time: 20 minutes
Cooking Time: 10 minutes

PORK FRIED RICE

2 cups	Minute Rice
5 Strips	Bacon (sliced)
3 Large	Green Onions (sliced)
1 Cup	Frozen Peas
3 Large	Mushrooms (thinly sliced)
2 Cups	Water
3 Tbsps.	Soya Sauce

1. Follow package instructions for rice
2. Fry bacon, dice and set aside
3. Fry mushrooms set aside
4. Add bacon, peas, soya sauce, and mushrooms to hot cooked rice mix thoroughly and serve

Prep Time: 10 minutes
Cooking Time: 15 to 20 minutes

CHICKEN CHOW MEIN

1 Pkg.	Chow Mein Noodles
1 Large	Chicken Breast (cubed)
3 Large	Green Onions (diced)
1 Cup	Bean Sprouts
1 Medium	Green Pepper (diced)
½ Medium	Red Pepper (diced)
3 Large	Mushrooms (sliced)
2 Cups	Chicken Broth
¼ Cup	Soya Sauce
1/3 Cup	Sesame Seed Oil

1. Pour oil in frying pan
2. Add vegetables except bean sprouts and stir fry until tender
3. Add the rest of ingredients except bean sprouts
4. Stir and cover on low heat for 15 to 20 minutes or until noodles are soft
5. Uncover and add bean sprouts toss and ready to serve

A FARE CHANCE

SUNDAY BRUNCH

SAVOURY BREAD PUDDING
MINI BLUEBERRY PANCAKES
PAN FRIES
BREAKFAST SAUSAGE
BANANA MUFFINS
QUICHE LORRAINE

Category: Entree
Servings: 4 to 6 Servings
Prep Time: 20 minutes
Cooking Time: 45 minutes
Serve with: Salad

SAVOURY BREAD PUDDING

4 Large	Eggs
¾ Cup	Crème
¼ Cup	Milk
2 Tbsp.	Dijon Mustard
1 Pound	Ground Stuffing Sausage
1 Loaf	Sourdough Bread (1-inch cubes)
1 Tbsp.	Green Onion (chopped)
¼ Cup	Red Pepper (diced)
¼ Cup	Mushrooms (diced)
1 Cup	Cheddar Cheese (shredded)
¼ Cup	Parmesan Cheese (shaved)

1. Toss cubed bread in bowl
2. Sauté vegetables until tender
3. Sauté sausage until brown
4. Whisk eggs, milk, cheese and mustard
5. Add sauté vegetables, sausage and egg mixture over bread cubes
6. Toss until bread is completely saturated
7. Pour into a buttered 8" square baking pan
8. Preheated 350° oven and place on middle rack
9. Bake for 45 minutes
10. Put a knife through the center of the pudding if it comes out clear, it's done

Prep Time: 10 minutes
Cooking Time: 12 to 15 minutes
Serve with: Sausages and eggs

MINI BLUEBERRY PANCAKES

2 Cups	Pancake Mix
1 Tsp.	Cinnamon Powder
1 Cup	Fresh Blueberries
½ Cup	Butter

1. Follow directions on pancake box
2. Add cinnamon and blueberries to pancake mix and blend
3. Melt butter to hot frying pan
4. Ladle the pancake mix of mini pancakes
5. When pancake begins to bubble flip pancake and cook for a minute or so
6. Continue this process until mix is finished
7. Serve with Butter and Maple Syrup

Prep Time: 5 minutes
Cooking Time: 15-20 minutes
Serve with: Quiche, Bacon & Eggs, Eggs & Salad

PAN FRIED POTATOES

2 Large	Russet Potato (diced)
1 Small	Onion (chopped)
1 Tbsp.	Seasoning Salt
3 Tbsps.	Canola Oil

1. Use non-stick frying pan
2. Add oil, potatoes, and onion
3. Sprinkle with Seasoning Salt
4. Let brown on one side before turning
5. Continue the process until potatoes are crisp and tender

Remember the ketchup, jam, and peanut butter.

Prep Time: 15 minutes
Cooking Time: 15 – 20 minutes
Serve with: Coffee, Fruit Salad

BANANA MUFFINS

2 Cups	Flour
½ Cup	Sugar
2 Tsps.	Baking Powder
½ Tsp.	Baking Soda
½ Tsp.	Salt
1 Tbsp.	Cinnamon
1 Cup	Raisins
2 Medium	Bananas (mashed chunky)
½ Cup	Milk
1/3 Cup	Oil
1 Large	Egg (slightly beaten)

1. Preheated 375° oven
2. Grease with butter 6 large cup muffin pan
3. Mix the first 6 ingredients in a bowl
4. Add the rest of the ingredients and fold until moisten
5. Spoon batter into each muffin cup filling 2/3 full
6. Bake on second oven rack for 15 to 20 minutes or until golden brown
7. Insert toothpick in center and if comes out clean muffin is done
8. Serve immediately

- Instead of banana you could use any berry like blueberries or strawberries.
- Instead of raisins you could use almonds or walnuts or any nut you like or both.
- Instead of banana add chopped onion, green pepper, bacon and shredded cheddar cheese.
- Instead of a cupcake recipe use this recipe by adding chocolate chips or soft candy or both along with food colouring and add icing of your choice.

Prep Time: 10 minutes
Cook Time: 35 minutes
Serve with: Salad and Potatoes, Muffins

QUICHE LORRAINE

1 9-Inch	Deep Dish Pie Crust Shell (prebaked)
4 Large	Eggs (Beaten)
1 ½ Cups	Light Cream
2 Tbsps.	Butter
6 Slices	Crisp Bacon (crumbled)
2 Cups	Swiss cheese (shredded)
¼ Cup	Green Onion (chopped)
¼ Cup	Green Pepper (chopped)
¼ Cup	Red Pepper (chopped)
¼ Cup	Mushrooms (thinly sliced)
1 Tbsp.	Dijon Mustard
1 Tbsp.	Worcestershire Sauce
1 Tsp.	Nutmeg (ground)

1. Preheated 350° oven
2. Bake pie crust following package instructions then cool
3. Cook Bacon strips and crumble
4. Melt butter add peppers and mushrooms cook until tender
5. Whisk eggs and milk in a large bowl
6. Add all ingredients and 1 cup of cheese to egg mixture then mix
7. Pour egg mixture into pie crust
8. Sprinkle remaining cheese over mixture
9. Bake for 35 to 40 minutes
10. Insert knife in center and if it comes out clean its ready to eat
11. Let stand for 5 minutes before serving

Variations:

Mushroom Quiche: Combine 1 cup sautéed sliced mushrooms, ½ cup sautéed onions, 1 cup cooked and drained spinach, 1 cup shredded white cheddar cheese, 1 cup shredded Parmesan Cheese, 1 tsp dried thyme, 1 tsp. pepper and seasoning salt.

Shrimp or Crab Quiche: Combine 1 cup shrimp or crabmeat, 1 cup shredded Gruyere cheese, 1 cup chopped red onion, 1 cup chopped red pepper, ½ cup chopped leeks, 1 tbsp. dried dill weed, 1 tbsp. dried parsley, and 1 tsp. pepper and seasoning salt.

A FARE CHANCE

FAMILY FARE DINNER

SOUTHERN FRIED CHICKEN
ROASTED POTATOES
BAKED GREEN BEAN CASSEROLE

Category: Entree
Servings: 2 to 4 Family Members/Friends
Prep Time: 10-15 minutes
Cooking Time: 30 minutes

SOUTHERN FRIED CHICKEN

8-10 pieces	Chicken
2 Large	Eggs (beaten)
4 Cups	Canola Oil
2 Cups	Flour
3 Tbsp.	Granulated Garlic
2 Tbsp.	Seasoning Salt
4	Popcorn kernels

1. Pour flour in a large Ziploc bag and set aside
2. Rinse chicken then toss in beaten eggs
3. Place chicken in bag of flour and toss until coated and set aside
4. Pour Oil in a large frying pan
5. Add 4 popcorn kernels to oil turn on high heat and wait for kernels to pop
6. Remove kernels and add in chicken skin face down in oil for 3 minutes
7. Turn chicken over and fry for 3 minutes
8. Take out and place on paper towel
9. Add to a roasting pan and season with garlic and salt
10. Place in preheated 350° oven and bake for 25 minutes
11. Serve immediately

Prep Time: 10 minutes
Cooking Time: 25 to 35 minutes

ROASTED POTATOES

4 large	Potatoes (eight cubes)
1 Cup	Butter (melted)

2 Tbsps.	Seasoning Salt
1 Tbsp.	Dill Weed (dry)
2 Tbsps.	Onion (dry minced)
2 Tbsps.	Garlic (dry minced)

1. Peel and cut potatoes into 8 cubes
2. Pour melted butter over the potatoes
3. Sprinkle the salt, dill, onion and garlic over potatoes
4. Place potatoes in a 350° oven for 25 to 35 minutes or until crisp and tender
5. Potatoes must be crispy on the outside to be ready

Prep Time: 10 minutes
Cooking Time: 30 minutes

BAKED GREEN BEAN CASSEROLE

2 (14 oz.) Cans	Cut Green Beans (drained)
½ Medium	Onion (diced)
½ Large	White Mushroom (finely sliced)
1/2 Cup	Sour Cream
3 Cups	Mozzarella (grated)
½ Cup	Butter (melted)
1 Cup	Breadcrumbs
3 Tbsps.	Flour
¾ Cup	Crème
1 Tbsp.	Garlic (granulated)
1 Tbsp.	Seasoning Salt

1. Drain the can of green beans pour into 8x4 loaf pan
2. In frying pan pour in half the butter add onions and mushrooms then fry until tender
3. Add flour to butter and vegetables stir into a paste
4. Add crème and whisk until slightly thicken and pour onto green beans
5. Add sour cream, cheese, garlic, and salt then toss until blended
6. Add breadcrumbs to rest of butter and mix until saturated
7. Sprinkle breadcrumbs over green beans
8. Bake preheated 350° oven for 30 minutes
9. Ready to serve

INFAMOUS ROAST BEEF DINNER

ROAST BEEF
BUTTERED BABY POTATOES
TURNIP & CARROT MASH
YORKSHIRE PUDDING
& GRAVY

Category: Entree
Servings: 6 to 8 servings
Prep Time: 10 minutes
Cooking Time: 1 to 2 hours

ROAST BEEF

4 lb.	Inside or Outside Beef Roast
3 Tbsp.	Liquid Smoke
2 Tbsp.	Dijon Mustard
1 Tbsp.	Granulated Garlic
1 Tbsp.	Onion Powder
1 Tbsp.	Thyme (dry)
1 Tbsp.	Seasoning Salt
2 Tbsp.	Black Pepper
1 Med.	Onion (thinly sliced)
4 Large	Mushrooms (thinly sliced)
3 Cups	Water

1. Blend liquid smoke and mustard together
2. Rub mustard mix over roast
3. Mix garlic, onion, thyme, salt and pepper
4. Sprinkle seasoning mix over roast
5. Pour water in roasting pan
6. Place roast in roasting pan
7. Place onion and mushrooms around the roast
8. Bake roast in preheated 350° oven
9. Roast at 15 minutes a pound for medium rare add 15 minutes for well-done
10. Remove from oven
11. Remove Roast from roasting pan and set pan aside for gravy
12. Let roast rest for 10 to 15 minutes before carving

Prep Time: 10 minutes
Cooking Time: 20 minutes

BUTTERED BABY POTATOES

Prep Time: 10 minutes
Cooking Time: 15 to 20 minutes

2 Pounds	Baby Potatoes
½ Cup	Butter (melted)
½ Cup	Green Onions (chopped)
1 Tsp.	Seasoning Salt
1 Tsp.	Black Pepper

1. Rinse potatoes
2. Add potatoes to pot of water
3. Boil until tender and drain
4. Add butter and green onions then toss
5. Leave on simmer for not more than 10 minutes before serving
6. Or if you want crispy add another 10 minutes to each side of potatoes

Prep Time: 10 minutes
Cooking Time: 20 minutes

TURNIP AND CARROT MASH

1 Small	Turnip (peeled & cubed)
4 Large	Carrots (peeled & sliced)
½ Cup	Butter (melted)
1 Tsp.	Seasoning Salt
1 Tsp.	Pepper

1. Prepare vegetables as above
2. Add carrots and turnip to pot of water
3. Boil until tender
4. Mash vegetables
5. Add butter, salt, pepper, and mix well
6. Ready to serve

Prep Time: 10 minutes
Cooking Time: 30 minutes

YORKSHIRE PUDDING

3 Large	Eggs
1 ½ Cup	Milk
1 ½ Cup	Flour
1 Tsp.	Salt
½ Cup	Vegetable or Canola Oil
1	12 x 9 baking pan

1. Morning of your dinner start preparing pudding
2. In a medium bowl whisk eggs, milk, flour and salt until smooth
3. Refrigerate until preparing dinner
4. Pour oil in 12 x 9-inch baking pan
5. Bake pan of oil in preheated 400° oven for 2 minutes
6. Remove pan from oven and quickly pour batter filling 2/3 full
7. Bake until pudding until golden brown about 30 minutes.
8. Slice into 8 equal pieces and serve immediately

Prep Time: 5 minutes
Cooking Time: 10 minutes

GRAVY

All Beef Drippings
2 Tbsp. Worcestershire Sauce
2 Tbsp. Package Gravy
1 Cup Water

1. Add water to beef drippings
2. Heat to boil roast beef drippings
3. Don't remove onions or mushrooms
4. Pour Sauce into drippings
5. Follow package instructions on Gravy mix
6. Medium to high heat cook until gravy thickens and bubbles
7. Ready to serve

FOOD FOR THOUGHT

APPETIZERS

I had given you nine of many favourites I've prepared over the years whether entertaining family, friends and clients when I had my catering & event business.

Have you ever wondered why appetizers came about? There is a history about these little bites, but first, let me give you some aliases over the decades. Let's start with hors d'oeuvre, canapé, appetizer, finger food, cocktail, tidbit, and now the starter. There have been others, but I think you get my point.

History has it that appetizers started as far back as the Romans and Greeks. Well, lounging they would have trays of foods to nibble on continuously throughout the day before serving a massive dinner of the same. In the time of the Renaissance, physicians advocated consuming tiny pieces of sodium prepared meats so to get their digestive systems ready for the main course and to ensure proper digestion.

Now, of course, we know the French had something to do with this.

Voilà they did! During the 17th century, the wealthy would pick at an arrangement of bite-sized foods; sometimes, even their dinners would present themselves in the same manner. The French called this service; a la française meaning French-style or fashion. I believe it was the French who came up with the name hors d'oeuvre which means 'outside the work' quite appropriate because hors d'oeuvres should not be part of the ordinary set of courses in a meal.

We can't forget the United States and Britain in this historical reflection they had to be part of this in some way or another. The influence of Europe's culinary habits began around 1860 in both these countries. And then there was Prohibition liking secretive cocktail parties where they would serve hors d'oeuvres to slow down the process of intoxication. The British liked the reasoning and adopted this form of eating into their culinary habits.

I bet you're wondering about us, Canadians? I'm not sure, and there's not much research; it's rather vague. I know from the fifties until the nineties hors d'oeuvres was what you served with cocktails before sitting for dinner, and an appetizer was your first course before your entrée. Today, formal dining has kept to this culinary presentation

SOUPS

Researchers think soup dates to the Neanderthal man, that's like around 200,000 to 28,000 years ago. Neanderthal man would boil the fat from his kill and then drink it.

You'll never guess where the word soup came from; the French? They had a winner, and they're undoubtedly excellent at branding food. I believed in the 16th century; a restaurant named their broth soup. But, in 1765, a Parisian entrepreneur opened a shop specializing in just soups. We all know the infamous French Onion Au Gratin, Vichyssoise, and Lobster Bisque which originated from of course France. I visited Paris last year, and the food was almost too American, but you can find intimate parts of Paris where you can smell the aromas of French cooking.

I believe the Germans are one of the best when it comes to soup preparation. In the 1880s, Germans had an appreciation for soups prepared with beer as a primary ingredient, and they still do. Noodles have been partnered with broth-based soups as early as the 1200s in Asia. Beginning in the 1700s in Italy, folks started feeding noodle soup to the sick because it was easy to digest. By the 1900s in the US, noodle soups had become a staple convenience food. In 1934, Campbell's "Noodle with Chicken Soup" debuted, thanks to creator Ernest Lacoutiere, a chef at the Campbell's company.

DESSERTS

Here we go with the French again, once again around the 16th century derived from the French word; desservir meaning clear the table, in France once all the dishes and cutlery were removed and only then could dessert be served. Then came the Industrial Revolution in the 19th century the apparent time for mass production of cakes and jellies. Did you know that eating desserts could help your digestive system say, Norwegian researchers?

One dessert most of us enjoy is ice cream, it was invented by the Chinese as far back as 3000 BC it started as flavoured ice and by the 1800s flavoured ice turned into ice cream. The American colonists loved pies, and I believe this; everyone has their favourite pie. It seems with men pumpkin, and apple pie seems to be their favourites. Did you know the first printed recipe was apple pie back in 1381?

Also, the name pumpkin originated from the Greek word Pepon. Pumpkin pie is famous in North America but not so anywhere else in the world. The first pumpkin pie originated with the early colonists, and it was their pie of choice for Thanksgiving. Dessert is a world tradition from India to Mexico you will always find dessert on the table but why at the end of your meal? Persians had it at the end of their meal to settle their stomachs.

SALADS

The five basic types of salad are green salads (tossed or composed), bound, vegetable, fruit, and combination. The five basic salads that can be served throughout a meal are starter, side, entree, break, and dessert. The salad has existed since ancient times. As an American food, salads were relatively insignificant until the nineteen sixties when there was a movement for natural and healthy. This was quite the change of events being the North American continent was about meat and potatoes. Regarding when to serve your salad well, it comes down to personal preference. In some cultures, you eat the salad at the end and in others at the beginning of the meal or during your meal.

I remember when lime jellied salads were a big rave in the fifties and sixties although it appeared in 1930 and of course just a footnote Mayonnaise made its appearance in 1915. The American salad of choice back then was iceberg lettuce, and it's still one of my favourites. The favourite dressings for salads at that time were Green Goddess, Thousand Island, Oil & Vinegar, and French. The salad bar showed up around 1940 but became popular in the seventies, especially in the steak houses or restaurants.

Of course, there is the infamous Caesar Salad was named after Caesar Cardini, who was an Italian born chef who immigrated to the United States after World War I. The Cardini family operated a restaurant in Tijuana, Mexico, primarily because of prohibition.

I love salad; I have a salad every day! You can make anything into a salad whether you have a combination of greens, vegetables, kinds of pasta, fruits and in some salads, you can add meat or seafood --- the same with salad dressings from cream based to oil based. Creating a salad is whatever you want it to be. Salads are great no matter the time of the year or the occasion.

Done!

Bon Appetit

www.ingramcontent.com/pod-product-compliance
Lightning Source LLC
Chambersburg PA
CBHW060423010526
44118CB00017B/2333